DOCTRINE OF THE GODHEAD

A Study of the Father, Son and Holy Spirit

J.J. Turner, D. Min., Ph. D.
&
Edward P. Myers, D. Min., Ph. D.

Solutions 2.0, Inc.

DEDICATION

To Our Wives
Isabel Turner and **Janice Myers**
They have stood patiently behind us during the
writing of this book
and all other efforts in His service.

Order From
Amazon.com

PREFACE OF SECOND EDITION

It is with a great deal of pleasure that I write a preface for the second edition of this book. First released in 1973, the book sold out within a few short years and has been out of print. Since that time, nothing fundamental has changed in our thinking related to this subject. Restudy has only to confirm what has already been stated here. The material in this printing has been completely re-typeset. The only changes made have been for spelling errors found in the first printing and a change in the format for consistency in footnotes. The authors would like to express appreciation to Mr. Bennie Whitehead and Quality Publications for bringing this material back into print.

This material has been well-received and used for classes in the local church, Christian Colleges, and Schools of Preaching. For the good it has accomplished in assisting in a study of this magnificent subject, we are thankful. We do not claim that this material is exhaustive, but only that it gives an overview to one of the most important subjects in Sacred Scripture. It is written primarily for the man in the pew. To our knowledge, there has been no other attempt in recent years for a study book written by anyone in our brotherhood. We do not want to seem presumptuous and say this is the last word on the matter. Our hope is that this material is beneficial to all who use it.

Edward P. Myers, Ohio Valley College Fall, 1984

CONTENTS

Introduction to the Godhead Study (7)
Grounds For Belief In God (17)
The Nature of God As Revealed In His Names (27)
The Essence of God (41)
The Triune Godhead (53)
Attributes of God (1) (63)
Attributes of God (2) (75)
The Pre-Existence and Deity of Christ (93)
The Incarnation of Christ (103)
The Resurrection of Christ (113)
The Holy Spirit of God (127)
The Holy Spirit in the Testaments (137)
The Holy Spirit Today (149)

Chapter One
INTRODUCTION TO GODHEAD STUDY
The Importance of the Study

The importance of any study is determined by some of the following things:

(1) The nature of the subject matter. What is it about?
(2) The relevancy of the subject to everyday life and needs.
(3) The benefits of the study. What will I gain personally? Will it make me wiser, happier, smarter, safer, better, etc.?
(4) One's previous interest in the subject. Will this study continue to build upon a previous background that I now want to enlarge?
(5) Curiosity about the subject. This attitude may stem from wanting to know only a few facts, not because one is really interested in the study for personal gain or needs.
(6) To prove or disprove a point (or teaching).
(7) Will there be any adverse effects from not having made the study?

Will there be a loss or penalty to me personally?

(8) Is the study a real challenge? Does it have a depth that will call upon all my abilities?

The Godhead study qualifies as important subject matter. The importance and magnitude of the Godhead study is beyond human comprehension. It is the greatest subject the human mind can pursue. This doctrine is the focal point of all right thinking, whether in the material or spiritual realm. A proper understanding provides the proper incentive for right, virtuous living in all societies. Even scientific progress, if it is to reach its greatest heights, is dependent upon a belief in God and a proper concept of His attributes. A proper concept of God is also the basis for peace and happiness within society and the individual. One has but to consider the harm which atheism, communism, and other no-god philosophies have caused, to see the great need for knowing God. Humanity suffers when God is left out.

Spurgeon in a sermon on Malachi 3:6, made the following comment on the importance of the Godhead study:

"Nothing will so enlarge the intellect, nothing so magnify the whole soul of man, as a devout, earnest, continued investigation of the great subject of the Deity. The most excellent study for expanding the soul is the science of Christ and Him crucified and the knowledge of the Godhead in the glorious Trinity. The proper study of the Christian is the Godhead. The highest science, the loftiest speculation, the mightiest philosophy, which can engage the attention of a child of God, is the name, the nature, the person, the doings, and the existence of the great God which he calls his Father. There is something exceedingly improving to the mind in a contemplation of the Divinity. It is a subject so vast, that all our pride is drowned in its infinity. Other subjects we can comprehend and grapple with; in them we feel a kind of self-content, and go on our way with the thought, "Behold I am wise." But when we come to this master science, finding that our plumb line cannot sound its depth, and that our eagle eye cannot see its heights, we turn away with the thought, "I am but of yesterday and know nothing." [1]

Jesus made it clear that eternal life is based upon a proper knowledge of God. He said, "And this is eternal life, that they know thee, the only true God, and Jesus Christ whom thou hast sent" (John 17:3). Many have overlooked this important condition of eternal life. The salvation of one's soul is based upon a proper understanding and belief in Jesus Christ as the Son of God (John 3:16; 10:10; 14:6; 20:30,31; Hebrews 5:9). This reason alone would be sufficient for studying the Godhead.

The Godhead study is important because of the many misunderstandings that exist, and are being taught, about Deity. This is true among world religions, cults, and denominationalists. Some view God as just a "Cosmic Force" in the universe. Others view the Holy Spirit as "it," or a mystical impersonal force. Jesus is viewed by some as "a god," and not an equal member of the Godhead. Some see Him as just a good man and teacher, but not Divine. The Pantheist sees God in nature, etc. Many New Testament Christians have a narrow concept of God because they have not studied this subject as they should. How about you?

The Godhead study is important because of the many questions that Christians and non-Christians have about God. Some of these questions are: Where is God? Where did God come from? Why should we believe in God? Can we really know God? Why doesn't God do something? Is God really dead? How do you explain three Gods in One? Isn't God in every man? Is Jesus God? Can you prove there is a God? Can you explain the Holy Spirit? Isn't God everywhere? Why does God permit evil? These are but a few of the many questions that people are asking about God, Christ and the Holy Spirit today. No doubt you have asked a similar question at one time or another. The fact that people are asking questions about God should prove that we must study in order to provide an answer: "But sanctify in your hearts Christ as Lord: being ready always to give answer to every man that asketh you a reason concerning the hope that is in you, yet with meekness and fear" (1 Peter 3:15). We are also commanded to study to show ourselves approved unto God (II Timothy 2:15). Therefore, we should want to study this important Bible doctrine.

Results of Leaving God Out:

The apostle Paul gives us the end results of losing the proper concept and knowledge of God:

Because that, knowing God, they glorified him not as God, neither gave thanks; but became vain in their reasonings, and their senseless heart was darkened. Professing themselves to be wise, they became fools, and changed the glory of the incorruptible God for the likeness of an image of corruptible man, and of birds, and four-footed beasts, and creeping things. Wherefore,

God gave them up in the lusts of their hearts unto uncleanness, that their bodies should be dishonored among themselves: for that they exchanged the truth of God for a lie, and worshipped and served the creature rather than the Creator, who is blessed for ever. Amen (Romans 1:21-25).

How sad for man to reduce God to his own image, or the image of birds, four-footed beasts, and creeping things.

Originally man had a natural sense of the one eternal God, his own Creator and the Creator of the entire universe. Then this natural sense became adulterated, corrupted. Historically, this corruption has expressed itself in (1) animism, (2) fetishism, (3) nature worship, (4) idolatry (worship of manufactured idols), (5) worship of man (some powerful individual^, (6) deification of the State, and (7) the dead-end results: atheism.

What a graphic picture of what will happen when men fail to maintain a proper concept of God, and serve Him accordingly.

Improper Concepts:

Paul, in his address to the Athenian philosophers, said, "Being then the offspring of God, we ought not to think that the Godhead is like unto gold, or silver, or stone, graven by art and device of men" (Acts 17:29). In the midst of idols of every description, the apostle admonished his hearers to develop a proper concept of the Godhead.

"There are variable concepts of God among the people of earth. They range from the crude, hazy and imperfect ideas of pagan people to the clear and correct view that God is the Supreme, Absolute and Infinite Personality who is the First Cause."

Our concept of God will determine how we worship and serve Him. Our concept of God is influenced and developed by many things. Note some of the following things that contribute to our concept of God:

(1) Our religious background is a very strong molding factor, and it

is hard for a man to break away from it in later years.
(2) Our concept of God is also based upon the teachings we have heard about God. This teaching may have come from various sources through the years. Such teachings may contain contradictions and, therefore, cause only confusion.
(3) Our social background may contribute to our concept of God. The home, school, acquaintances, etc., are strong influences upon us all.
(4) Our educational background (college, etc.) will contribute to our concept of God. Teachers have a strong influence over their students. Some are atheists today because their favorite teacher was one.
(5) Trials, misfortunes, troubles, resentments, prejudices, etc., also contribute to our concept of God.
(6) Our concept or bias toward God may be formed out of an ungodly attitude and practice of sin. This is why many want to rule God out of their thoughts and lives.

There are many other factors that help to mold our concept of God. These, however, will serve to illustrate the point that many things contribute to our concept of God.

Many today who claim to believe in the true God of the Bible have a warped, inaccurate concept of Him. Some view God as:

The God who is in the image of one's earthly father. If their father was mean or cruel, they think of the Heavenly Father as being the same way. After all, aren't they both fathers?

The God who carries a little black book. He is standing by just hoping that you will make a mistake, so He can place a check mark by your name.

The God of the local church. He is not concerned or involved with anything beyond the church building. If you need Him, you must go there to find Him.

The God who is on vacation. He never seems to be around when you need Him.

The God who is out of date. He doesn't understand the modern needs, problems and way of life.

The God who wound the universe up and has stepped out of the picture to let it run down.

The God of confusion. He doesn't know what He wants. (People especially reach this conclusion after viewing the maze of denominationalism.)

The God who is always demanding, and never giving. His demands are always against what I want.

The God who doesn't want anybody to have fun. He is very strict and is always saying, "Thou shalt not."

The God of the privileged few. The poor man may think that God is only on the rich man's side. Many see God as the God of only a certain race, etc.

The God who is equal to man; therefore, He has no right to tell man what to do.

The God who arbitrarily inflicts people with many horrible diseases which must be accepted as the will of God.

The man who has a proper concept of God will serve Him out of love, understanding, and respect. Even though he may not fully understand why God requires a certain thing, he knows that God loves him and seeks only his higher good. He is motivated to keep the commandments of Jesus because of love and understanding (John 14:15). The redeemed man will be active in the local church because he knows in **whom** he has believed (II Timothy 1:12). With all warped concepts removed, he now knows the Father as he should. He believes, as Paul did, "that God is able..." (Ephesians 3:20; II Timothy 1:12).

Source of Study:

It should be clear from the very beginning that our main source of material for the Godhead study will come from the Bible. The Bible is God's book—His record—about Himself and His dealings with mankind. It is in His book that we will find the answers to all our questions, not only about Him, but about ourselves, too. This study is based upon the assumption that each student believes in the verbal, plenary inspiration of the Scriptures. Paul said:

Every scripture inspired of God is also profitable for teaching, for reproof, for correction, for instruction which is in righteousness: that the man of God may be complete, furnished completely unto every good work (II Timothy 3:16,17).

Jesus said, "And ye shall know the truth, and the truth shall make you free" (John 8:32). He also informs us that His words are truth (John 17:17). Therefore, the Bible is a safe guide to follow in our study.

In our study, we will also use the works of various scholars. What a wonderful privilege to glean from the years of study that others have made in our subject area. Our goal in using the Scriptures and the works of men is to know the truth about this important subject. The student is encouraged to supplement this study guide with any other works that may contribute to his understanding of this great doctrine.

Some Definitions:

The meanings of words are important. This is especially true in the Godhead study, and things related to this important doctrine. From time to time, as we study and try to teach others, we are confronted with words that may confuse us if we do not know their meaning. Familiarity with the following words will help you as you study and teach this important subject:

Agnostic... One who believes that God, life, hereafter, etc., can neither be proven nor disproven, and who accepts material phenomena only.

Atheism... The belief that there is no God.

Anthropomorphism... The using of human attributes to describe God.

Asceticism... The practice of severe self-discipline and austerity, in the belief that this will assist spiritual progress.

Deism... The belief, on purely rational grounds, without revelation, in the existence of God.

Dualism... The belief that there are two independent principles in the universe as, for instance, good and evil.

Materialism... The belief that nothing exists but matter and its movements and modifications.

Monism... The belief that there is but one Being in the universe.

Monotheism... The belief that there is only one God.

Mysticism... Spiritual apprehension of truth by means beyond the reason and understanding.

Pantheism... The belief that God is everything and everything is God.

Polytheism... The belief that there are many gods.

Theism... Belief in a God who has been revealed to man.

Trinity... Belief in one God manifested in three personalities.

Tritheism... Belief in three Gods who have formed a union.

Our Objectives:

In our introduction so far, we have tried to establish the need and importance of the Godhead study. In our study of the Godhead, we will try to increase our understanding of God, and thereby avoid many of the problems that come from a limited or warped concept. A proper understanding of this important subject will increase our faith and trust in God. As our faith and trust increase, so shall our joy and happiness in His service increase. One objective, therefore, of this study is to encourage us to serve God out of love, trust, and reverence. This service will stem from knowing that we are serving the only true and living God, Who is able to do all things.

In our study of the Godhead, we will notice some of the reasons for believing in God. Then we will study the essence and attributes of God. We will also study the Deity of Jesus Christ and His relationship to the Godhead. The Holy Spirit of the Godhead will also be studied. A proper understanding of the Father, Son, and Holy Spirit is imperative to an understanding of the Godhead. This approach will help us to know the true and living God, as He should be known by His creation.

At the end of each lesson, there is a series of questions for class discussion. These are designed to encourage a study of the lesson guide before class, and thus prepare each student for an open discussion of the subject in the classroom. May God bless you as you learn more about Him during the next few weeks, and the remainder of your life.

QUESTIONS FOR DISCUSSION
Memorize John 17:3 (write out in class).

1. Write a paragraph about your present concept of God. (Use separate sheet of paper and bring to class for discussion.)
2. Has anyone ever asked you a question about God? Discuss some of them.
3. Why is it important to answer people? What should we do if we do not know the answer?
4. What determines the importance of any study?
5. Why is the Godhead study important?
6. Discuss John 17:3.
7. Give some additional false concepts of God, which many hold.
8. What one factor has influenced your concept of God the most?
9. What motivates you the most to serve God?
10. Why should the Bible be our main source for studying the Godhead?
11. Review and discuss some of the definitions.

12. What do you hope to gain from this study?

FOOTNOTES

[1] C. H. Spurgeon, *The Park Street Pulpit* (Grand Rapids, MI: Zondervan Publishing House, 1856), p. 1.

[2] John Clover Monsma, *The Evidence of God In an Expanding Universe* (New York, NY: G. P. Putman's Sons, 1958), p. 13.

[3] J. J. Keyser, *A System of Natural Theism,* pp. 11-12.

Chapter Two
GROUNDS FOR BELIEF IN GOD

Introduction

The existence of God is the first truth assumed in the Bible: "In the beginning God" (Genesis 1:1). There is no formal attempt, as in other religions, to prove the origin or existence of God. This approach is especially unique when we consider the environment in which Moses wrote these words. Geikie describes this environment: "The Egyptian theology, amidst which Moses had grown up, dwelt on the birth of the gods from Osiris, and told how he, the sun, brought forth the seven great planetary gods, and then the twelve humbler gods of the signs of the Zodiac; they, in their turn, producing the twenty-eight gods presiding over the stations of the moon, the seventy-two divine companions of the sun, and other deities." [1] Thus in the midst of a world that believed in many gods, Moses, by. inspiration from God, declares in Genesis, chapters one through three, that there is **one** All- Powerful God, Who created the heavens and earth and all things therein, and Who revealed Himself to Adam and Eve, the first male and female. Paul argued that all men, at one time, knew the only true God of Heaven (Romans 1:21-28).

The obvious question is: What has happened to this belief and knowledge of God through the ages? There are literally thousands, or perhaps millions, today who share the expression of the man described by the Psalmist of old: "The fool hath said in his heart, There is no God" (Psalm 14:1). The atheists of today are saying, "There is no God!" The skeptic is saying, "I am not sure that God does exist." And the agnostic is saying, "We can't really know whether or not a God does exist." Moving from these extreme expressions, all men at one time or another have asked, "Does God exist?"; "How can I be sure that there is a God?"; etc. Therefore, in our study of the Godhead, it will be helpful for us to examine some of the reasonable proofs for believing in God. The study of the Godhead is based upon a belief in God.

It is not possible, in the final analysis, to **prove** from empirical observation that God does exist. This is true because the Essence of God is Spirit (John 4:24). Therefore He cannot, as Spirit, be seen with the human eye. The purpose of this lesson, therefore, will be to examine reasonable proofs which serve as pointers for believing in the existence of God.

Some Reasons for Belief in God

There have been many arguments, through the years, set forth to prove the existence of a Supreme Being. Some of these have been weak, and others have been strong. Notice some of the following arguments.

The Anthropological Argument. This argument is based upon the universal belief in a Supreme Being. Archaeological research has established that all nations, in every place, during every age, have practiced some kind of religion and worshipped something or someone as supreme above themselves. It is obvious that the universal belief in a deity had to come from somewhere. Where did these beliefs come from? What made man decide to bow down and worship?

Man could not invent, or originate the idea of a God, a Spirit, a future state, or any positive institutions of religion; he could never have invented or originated the ideas inseparably connected with the words priest, altar, sacrifice, etc.; ergo, that these ideas and the words used to express them, are derivable only from an immediate and direct revelation; men have no power according to any philosophic analysis of his intellectual powers, to originate any such ideas. [2] Therefore, man did not invent the idea of God. It came by revelation from God. (Read again Romans 1:20-28.)

Man is incurably religious. No nation or tribe of people has been discovered that does not believe in some kind of Supreme Being, and practice some form of religion. We may go farther and say that, in all the religions of the earth there are traces of monotheism—belief in one God. No matter how polytheistic we find a people, nor how deeply enshrouded in darkness their religion is, there are always faint, glimmering rays of a purer light. In the midst of the belief in many gods, we find relics of the faith of a previous time—a purer monotheism. It is also worthy of note that the earlier forms of the various heathen religions are purer than the later forms. Principal Fairbain, of Oxford, lays down the general rule with regard to historical religions: 'The younger the polytheism, the fewer its gods.' [3]

In any discussion about the existence of God, the argument from universal belief must be considered. This argument, which is supported by archaeological research, agrees with the Bible account of man's knowing the one true God, and then wandering from Him into lower forms of idolatry.

The Cosmological Argument. This is an argument from first cause. It is based upon the belief that every effect in the universe has behind it an adequate cause. In a broader sense, Cosmology is a theory or philosophy which deals with the nature and principles of the universe. One of the first men to use this argument was Thomas Aquinas (A.D. 1224-1274). Aquinas, in his *Summa Theologica,* part 1, question 2, article 3, offers five ways to prove the Divine existence. The argument begins by observing some feature in the universe (e.g., planets, stars, order, etc.), and then arguing for a first cause for the production of that which is observable—something cannot come from nothing. John Hick breaks this argument down into the following points:

(1) "The first way argues from the fact of motion to a Prime mover."
(2) "The second from causation to a first cause."
(3) "The third from contingent beings to a necessary being."
(4) "The fourth from degrees of value to absolute value."
(5) "The fifth from evidences of purposiveness in nature to a divine." [4]

The Cosmological argument is worthy of discussion and use. It should be pointed out, however, that since the days of Hume, this argument has been rejected by most philosophers (which doesn't mean too much, one way or another, because they must still deal with a first cause). Strong sums up the value of this argument:

It proves the existence of some cause in the universe indefinitely great. When we go beyond this and ask whether this cause is a cause of being, or merely cause of change, to the universe, or with it; whether it is intelligent or unintelligent, infinite or finite, one or many—this argument cannot assure us. [5] For the Christian, it is reasonable to believe that the first cause is God.

The Teleological Argument. Teleos is the Greek word for **end** or **purpose.** The Teleological argument is based upon the design and purpose in the universe. Design calls for a designer. This approach, in the philosophical realm, has been used from the time of Plato's *Timaeus.* It appears, also, in Thomas Aquinas' works. William Paley (A.D. 1743-1805) uses this argument in his works on Natural Theology.

By design is intended: (1) The selection of an end to be attained, (2) The choice of suitable means for its attainment, and (3) the actual application of those means for the accomplishment of the proposed end. Such being the nature of design, it is a self- evident truth, or, even an identical proposition, that design is indicative of intelligence, will, and power. It is simply saying that intelligence in the effect implies intelligence in the cause. It is moreover true that the intelligence indicated by design is not the thing designed. It must be an external agent.

A careful study of the Teleological argument will reveal, perhaps, that this is the strongest philosophical argument favoring the existence of God. The universe reflects system and a high degree of organization. It is obvious that blind chance or mere accident never built anything. The All-Wise God of heaven created the earth to be inhabited by man: "For thus saith Jehovah that created the heavens, the God that formed the earth and made it, that established it and created it not a waste, that formed it to be inhabited: I am Jehovah; and there is none else" (Isaiah 45:18). Therefore, everything in the universe is there for a purpose (Isaiah 40:12), and demonstrates God's Power and Wisdom in design. The probability of life and design originating from accident is comparable to the Unabridged Dictionary resulting from an explosion in a printing shop, or the pouring out of a can of alphabet soup into alphabetical order.

The Hebrew writer said, "Now faith is the substance of things hoped for, the evidence of things not seen" (Hebrews 11:1). The Psalmist said, "...And the heavens are the works of thy hands" (Psalm 102:25). Therefore, "The heavens declare the glory of God; and the firmament showeth his handiwork" (Psalm 19:1). Order, design, purpose and harmony exist in the universe because God created it unto this end.

The Ontological Argument. This is a very difficult philosophical argument from Metaphysics. It is based upon the nature of God's being. Anselm, in the eleventh and twelfth centuries, expressed the argument in the following way: "The idea of perfection included existence; for that which does not exist will be less than perfect; therefore, since we have the idea of a perfect being, that being must exist; for the idea includes his being or he would be less than perfect." In simple language, this argument means that God exists because we have the concept of His existence in our mind; and this concept is that He is a Perfect Being. The idea of perfect must have a first cause.

The Moral Argument. This argument is based upon the fact that all men have a sense of right and wrong. Some try to discredit this argument by calling it an instinct. If it is an instinct (like birds flying south), where did it come from? Again we come to a First cause. Man's moral awareness is a quality of the human spirit, planted in him by God. Therefore, there is reason to argue for the existence of

God, based upon the moral awareness of all men. Where did this awareness come from, if it was not placed within man by the All-Wise Heavenly Father? Paul said, "For when the Gentiles that have not the law do by nature the things of the law, these, not having the law, are the law unto themselves; in that they show the work of the law written in their hearts, their conscience bearing witness therewith, and their thoughts one with another accusing or else excusing them" (Romans 2:14,15).

The Bibliology Argument. This argument offers proofs from the Bible for the existence of God. Such passages as Genesis chapters one through three, Exodus 3:13, Psalm 139:7-10, Isaiah46:10, and Malachi 3:6, etc., are used in an appeal to prove the existence of God. The uniqueness of the Bible is also used as proof for God's existence; e.g., written by approximately forty men over a period of sixteen hundred years, yet without contradictions, and telling one story. How can you explain this uniqueness without a Supreme Designer behind it? Prophecy and its fulfillment are also another strong proof for the existence of God. Note the following prophecies: concerning Egypt—Isaiah 19 and Ezekiel 29:30; concerning Nineveh—Isaiah 10:12-14 and Zephaniah 2:13-15; concerning Babylon—Isaiah 13:1-14 and Jeremiah 50-51; concerning Christ—Micah 5:2, cf. Matthew 2:1; Zechariah 9:9; cf. Matthew 21:4,5; 27:22,23; Isaiah 53:10,11 and 9:6,7, etc. Again, how can we account for these without a Supreme, All-Knowing God as the giver of prophecy? We cannot!

The Resurrection of Christ. This argument is based upon the historical, miraculous event of Christ's resurrection from the grave. The proving of this supernatural event proves the existence of a Supernatural Power behind the event. The importance of this event is seen in its being mentioned over one hundred times in the New Testament. (Read 1 Corinthians 15:1-5; 12-19.)

Homer Hailey makes the following comments on the effect of the resurrection: 1. On Mary: from a frustrated woman to a bringer of good news. 2. Peter: ran to the tomb. Concern for Jesus, or for forgiveness? 3. John: keen observer, believed. 4. Disciples: from fearful men to bold, courageous witnesses. 5. Thomas: the climax of evidence. From a skeptic to strongest belief: "My Lord and my God," and from a Jew! Possibly John's greatest human witness to the resurrection.

The resurrection of Christ, and the conversion of Saul of Tarsus, in this writer's opinion (plus Bibliology arguments), are the strongest proofs for belief in the existence of God. Each Christian would do well to learn these very vital arguments in proving the existence of God. (A study of Christian Evidences is a must.)

Argument From Personal Feelings. Those who use this type of argument when asked, "Why (or how) do you believe that there is a God?" usually reply, "Oh, I feel Him in my heart," or, "I talked to Him this morning," etc. This type of argument (it is not really an argument) has caused many people to laugh at believers in God. It should be obvious that this approach is very weak, and lacking in proof. On the same basis, an atheist could say, "I know that there isn't a God, because I feel it in my heart." The world is looking for (and in need of) evidences, not feelings. Feelings should cause one to arm himself with reasons!

Conclusion

Most of these arguments, except the ones from Bibliology and the resurrection, are limited in their scope. This does not mean, however, that they are not useful in presenting a reasonable case for belief in God. It would be well to remember, however, that these arguments provide **pointers;** they do not reveal a personal God who loves man. Therefore, today, God does not exist to point us to the Bible, but the Bible (and nature) points us to a Personal, All-Powerful, Sustaining God, who loves us and sent His only Begotten Son to die for us as a demonstration of that love.

REVIEW QUESTIONS:
1. Discuss the first truth assumed in the Bible.
2. How did men lose their knowledge of a personal God? Discuss.
3. Why can't we **prove,** without question or doubt, that there is a God?
4. Discuss the good points of the Anthropological argument. Where does its weakness lie?
5. Does everything demand a first cause? Discuss.
6. What impresses you the most in the design of the universe? Discuss.
7. Discuss Romans 2:14,15.
8. Why do we believe that the Bible is inspired? How does this relate to the existence of God?
9. Why is the resurrection of Christ important in proving God's existence? Discuss Saul's (Paul) conversion.
10. Discuss arguments from feelings.
11. Discuss "pointers."
12. How does proving the existence of God relate to a study of the Godhead?
13. Have you had a study in Christian Evidences?

FOOTNOTES

'Cunningham Geikie, *Hours With the Bible* (New York, NY: James Pott Pub. Co., 1884), Vol. 1, p. 21.

Alexander Campbell, *Campbell-Owen Debate: The Evidences of Christianity;* complete in one volume (Nashville: McQuiddy Printing Company, 1957 reprint).

'*Oliphant-Smith Debate* (Nashville, TN: Gospel Advocate Co., 1952), p. 5.

⁴John Hick, *Philosophy of Religion* (Englewood, NJ: Prentice-Hall, 1963), p. 20.

"A. Strong, *Systematic Theology* (Old Tappan, NJ: Fleming Revell

Co., 1907), pp. 74-75.

^Charles Hodge, *Systematic Theology* (Grand Rapids, MI: Wm, Eerd man Pub. Co.), Vol. 1, p. 216.

Homer Hailey, *Internal Evidences of Christianity* (Akron, OH: Evidences Quarterly, 1964), p. 54.

Chapter Three
THE NATURE OF GOD AS REVEALED IN HIS NAMES

Introduction

There was a time when a man's name told you a lot about that man. At one time, surnames indicated occupations (e.g., John Smith was usually a worker of metal; John Baker was a preparer of bread; George Miller was a grinder of grain; John Gardener was a man who took care of a garden; George Carpenter was a builder). Positions were known by names (e.g., John Earl, George Duke, etc.). Surnames also indicated a man's residence (e.g., John Britton, George London, etc.). A name would also indicate some attribute or event associated with the person (e.g., John Longfellow, George Drinkwater). Even today names still carry significant meanings, especially in determining a person's ancestral background, ethnic origin, or for legal purposes, etc. Some even change their names to more desirable names (movie stars, actors, writers, etc.).

Names, as used in the Bible, carried significant meanings. They often indicated a person's character or some peculiar quality (e.g., Adam means **red earth).** This has reference to the ground from which he was formed. Abraham means father of a **multitude.** This is in light of God's promise to save men through the seed of woman (Genesis 3:15). Jesus means **Savior** (Matthew 1:21). Peter means **Rock** (Matthew 16:18). David means **well beloved.** Isaac means **laughter,** etc.

In the Bible, especially in the Old Testament, God revealed Himself by several special names. These special names give us a deeper insight into the nature of God, and help us also to see His relationship to His creation. It was made clear that, "Thou shalt not take the name of the Lord thy God in vain" (Exodus 20:7).

The knowledge of God's name cannot be over-emphasized. The

Psalmist said, "They that know thy name will put their trust in thee" (Psalm 9:10). It is obvious that **one** name could not describe God's greatness. After all, as
one writer declares, "A name imposes some limitation. It means that an object or a person is this and not that, is here and not there. And if the heaven of heavens cannot contain God, how can a name describe Him?" Therefore, in this lesson, we will learn more about the attributes and glory of God by studying some of His names as revealed in the Bible. In a study of God's names, we will see more than ever before just how important a name really is.

Personal Names Elohim. The first name we find translated "God" in the Old Testament is **Elohim.** Its etymology is from **El** (Mighty One and All-Powerful One) and **Alah** (to swear, to make a covenant). The name conveys the idea of strength, creative and governing power, by the Almighty who keeps His promises. It occurs in Genesis, chapter one, thirty times and over two hundred times in the rest of the book. **Elohim** occurs 2570 times in the Old Testament. The word is a Hebrew masculine-ending noun, plural in form. Unless the word is used in reference to heathen gods (I Samuel 4:8), it is always joined, or governed by, a singular verb or adjective.

It is characteristic of Hebrew that extension, magnitude and dignity, as well as actual multiplicity, are expressed by the plural. It is not reasonable, therefore, to assume that plurality of form indicates primitive Sem Polytheism. On the contrary, historic Hebrew is unquestionably and uniformly monotheistic. ' Notice the singular pronoun accompanying the plural **Elohim: "I am [Elohim]** and there is no **[Elohim]** beside **me"** (Deuteronomy 32:39; Isaiah 45:5,22). In the following places, singular adjectives are used: Psalm 57:2; 7:9; II Kings 19:4,16.

In the very beginning of the Bible, therefore, we are introduced to the Omnipotent God Who created the heavens and earth and made a covenant with man. Moses makes it clear in the first two chapters of Genesis, by using **Elohim,** that this One God possessed the sum total of all the power which the heathen conceived (and even more) as being distributed among their many gods. (In chapter five we will study the triune nature of the Godhead.)

El. This is the most common name used for Deity. It is a generic term which expresses authority, strength, and majesty. From this root word is derived such words as **Elim, Eloah,** and **Elohim. El** is especially predominant in the books of Job and Psalms. It is frequently used with nouns or adjectives to form compound names which express a particular attribute of God's being **(El-roi, El-elyon).** Also, since it is a generic term, it is used to describe the authority, honor, and position among men (Moses was **Elohim** to Pharaoh, Exodus 8:1, and to Aaron, Exodus 4:16; cf. I Samuel 2:25; Judges 5:8; Psalm 58:11; 82:1).

El-elyon. This name denotes the God of Israel as the most high God. It distinguished Him from the pagan gods. **El-elyon,** alone, was Supreme and ruled heaven and earth:

And the king of Sodom went out to meet him after his return from the slaughter of Chedorlaomer, and of the kings that were with him, at the valley of Shaveh, which is the king's dale. And Melchizedek, king of Salem, brought forth bread and wine: and he was the priest of the most high God, possessor of heaven and earth: And blessed be the most high God, which hath delivered thine enemies into thy hand... (Genesis 14:17-20).

This is why Israel could have no other gods before them (Exodus 20:3). Jehovah was Supreme!

El-roi. This name denotes the God of heaven as the God who sees. This name was given to God by Hagar as she fled from Sarai, Abram's wife (Genesis 16:6). As Hagar sat alone in the wilderness trying to determine what to do next, an angel appeared unto her and said, "...I will greatly multiply thy seed, that it shall not be numbered for multitude. And the angel of Jehovah said unto her, Behold, thou art with child, and shall bear a son; and thou shall call his name Ishmael [God heareth, JJT], because Jehovah hath heard thy affliction...And she called the name of Jehovah that spake unto her, Thou art a God **[El-roi]** that seeth: for she said, Have I even here looked after him that seeth me? Wherefore the well was called Beer-La-hai-roi [the well of the living One who seeth]; behold, it is between Kadesh and Bered (Genesis 16:10-16).

Many years later **El-roi** said, as He was ready to deliver Israel from Egyptian bondage, "I have surely seen the affliction of my people that are in Egypt, and have heard their cry by reason of their taskmasters; for I know their sorrows" (Exodus 3:7). How wonderful to know, even today, that God sees and is mindful of all our troubles and afflictions. The Psalmist said, "Behold, the eye of Jehovah is upon them that fear him, Upon them that hope in his lovingkindness; To deliver their soul from death, And to keep them alive in famine" (Psalm 33:18,19).

We must always remember that the God of heaven sees every sin we commit (Jeremiah 13:22), and is "of purer eyes than to behold evil, and that canst not look on perverseness..." (Habakkuk 1:13). Therefore, if we continue in our sins, Jehovah will say, "I will cast you out of my sight..." (Jeremiah **7:15**). What does **[El-roi]** see in you? Remember, He never sleeps (Psalm 121:3).

El-shaddai. This name is translated "Almighty" in the English Bible. This name was especially known by the Patriarchs (Genesis 17:1,8,15,22; 18:9-14). **Shaddai** occurs forty-eight times in the Old Testament. The word is believed to be derived from a word that means "breast," which conveys the idea of one who is able to supply, nourish, and satisfy. Therefore, when **Shaddai** is connected with **El,** the meaning is that God is mighty to supply, nourish, and satisfy; He is all-bountiful and all-sufficient. No matter what Israel's needs were, He could meet them. Notice how **El-shaddai** is used in Genesis 49:24,25, concerning Joseph: "...the arms of his hands were made

strong by the hands of the mighty God of Jacob...even by the God [El] of thy father, who shall help thee; and by the Almighty **[Shaddai]**, who shall bless thee with blessings of heaven above, blessings of the deep that lieth under, blessings of the breasts and of the womb."
In Revelation 16:7, God is seen as the all-sufficient and all-bountiful One.

Adonai. Adonai is the plural form of **Adon.** The word means "Master," or "Lord." **Adonai** is used over three hundred times in the Old Testament. The word almost always agrees with the plural **Elohim,** because it appears in the plural and possessive, and means **my Lord.** Note Psalm 110:1: "Jehovah [singular] said unto my **[Adonai (plural)],** Sit thou at my right hand, until I make thine enemies thy footstool." (This prophecy refers to Christ, Acts 2:34,35. Therefore, we have Jehovah speaking to Christ in the Godhead.) **Adonai** is also translated "owner." Therefore, **Adonai** is the Master, Lord, and Owner of all (Deuteronomy 10:17). How wonderful to know that Christ is our Master today (Acts 9:6; Galatians 1:16,17; 6:17; I Timothy 1:12; Acts 20:24; Romans 6:16; I Corinthians 7:22).

Rock. This name denotes the steadfast, firm nature of God. He is a safe retreat (Psalm 94:22), a mighty fortress (Psalm 61:1), in time of need. The **Rock** (Hebrew **cur**) brought Israel forth out of bondage: "Of the Rock that begat thee thou art unmindful, and hast forgotten God that formed thee" (Deuteronomy 32:18). Christ, the Rock, followed Israel in the wilderness (I Corinthians 10:4). It was upon Christ, the Rock, that the church was built (Matthew 16:13-18).

Father. The name "Father" conveys the idea of begetter, sustainer, upholder, nourisher, and protector (basic idea of **El-shaddai).** Israel knew God as their Father: "Do ye thus requite the Lord, O foolish people and unwise, is not he thy father that hath bought thee? Hath he not made thee, and established thee?" (Deuteronomy 32:6). "Doubtless thou art our father..."
(Isaiah 63:16). "But now, O Lord, thou art our father; we are the clay,

and thou art our potter; and we all are the work of thy hand" (Isaiah 64:8).

Jesus came to reveal the Father more fully. He said, "...he that hath seen me hath seen the Father...I am in the Father, and the Father in me..." (John 14:7,9,10). (Read Psalm 103:13; Jeremiah 3:4,19; 31:9; Malachi 1:6; 2:10; Exodus 4:22; Hosea 1:10.)

Special or Covenant Name Jehovah. This name is used more than any other name for God in the Old Testament. We read it first in Genesis 2:4, where it is combined as **Jehovah-elohim.** It occurs in the Old Testament 6,823 times. The etymology of the word comes from the Hebrew verb **havah,** and means "to be," or "being." Israel's attention was called to the name in Exodus 3:13-15:

And Moses said unto God, behold, when I come unto the children of Israel, and shall say unto them, The God of your fathers hath sent me unto you; and they shall say to me, What is his name? What shall I say unto them? And God said unto Moses, **"I am that I am"**; and he said, Thus shall thou say unto the children of Israel...The Jehovah God of your fathers, the God of Abraham, the God of Isaac, and the God of Jacob, hath sent me unto you: this is my name forever and this is my memorial unto all generations. (See Exodus 6:2-4.)

"I am that I am" or "I shall be what I shall be" declares Jehovah's (also called "Yahweh") unchangeableness, not only of being, but also of relationship to His people.

Fitzwater gives the following breakdown of the phrase, **"I am that I am"**;

The Self-Existent One. "I am" implies the One who exists by Himself and is the cause of all existence.

The Self-Sufficient One. "I am that I am"—this means that the Divine Being does not go outside Himself to explain Himself. The fact is that there is no analogy in the range of human concept and experience to express this idea.

The Immutable One. There is no change in the nature of God, neither in His ways (Malachi 3:6).

Therefore, Israel had the Divine assurance that the Almighty would be with them. They were reminded of this every time they heard the name Jehovah uttered in their midst. It was the covenant-memorial name throughout their generations. (Read Revelation 1:4,8,17; 2:8; 21:6; 22:13.)

In the New Testament, Jesus claimed the title **"I am"** (John 8:58). In John 8:24, Jesus said we must believe that He is **"I am"** (the word **He** has been added). Since Jesus is **"I am,"** we have the assurance of our covenant (Matthew 26:28; Cf. Hebrews 13:20), too.

Compound Names of God:

As we have noted above, from Genesis 2:4 onward, Jehovah is the personal name that is constantly used for God. Jehovah is the eternal, all- sufficient, self-existent One. In the Old Testament, there are a number of names compounded with Jehovah. These compound names gave the chosen people a little deeper insight into God's nature, and what He was able to do for them in a very special way. A careful study of the following compound names will reveal that they arose out of some historical event, and picture Jehovah meeting Israel's every need. It is also wonderful to know that each of these compound terms is fully realized and revealed in Christ Jesus, our Saviour. Thus, again, if we have seen Him, we have seen the Father.

Jehovah-jireh. This compound name means, "Jehovah will provide." No matter what our needs may be, we can trust Jehovah-jireh to provide: "And Abraham called the name of that place **Jehovah-jireh:** as it is said to this day, in the mount of the Lord it shall be seen" (Genesis 22:14). In the greatest crisis of Abraham's life, he knew that God would provide.

God has provided His greatest gift to mankind—He has provided salvation for us through Christ—"The Lamb of God that taketh away the sin of the world" (John 1:29). Not only has He provided salvation,

Paul said, "But my God shall supply all your needs according to his riches in glory by Christ Jesus" (Philippians 4:19). God still provides today!

Jehovah-tsidkenu. This compound name means, "Jehovah our righteousness." **Tsidkenu** comes from the Hebrew **tsedek** (righteousness), and basically means straight or stiff. Many Hebrew scholars express the impossibility of properly translating the word by any one English word. The word is used hundreds of times in the Old Testament. It pictures God as dealing with men under the ideas of acquittal, justification, and righteousness. Notice its use in Jeremiah 33:16, "In those days shall Judah be saved, and Jerusalem shall dwell safely: and this is the name wherewith she shall be called, The Lord our righteousness" (Marginal: "Jehovah- tsidkenu").

Jehovah was the source of righteousness in the Old Testament. Today, under the New Testament, Christ is our righteousness: "For he hath made him to be sin for us, who knew no sin; that we might be made the righteousness of God in him" (II Corinthians 5:21).[1] Therefore, we appear righteous because of Christ's righteousness (Romans, chapter 4).

Jehovah-M. Kaddesh. This compound name means, "Jehovah who sanctifies." The word **holy** or **hallow** stands for that which is set apart. One scholar states that **sanctify,** in its various forms, appears over seven hundred times in the Old Testament (especially in Leviticus). In Exodus 13:2, the firstborn were set apart (or sanctified) for service unto God. In verse 12 of this same thirteenth chapter, we see certain animals set apart (or sanctified). Jehovah also set apart (sanctified) special days, feasts, utensils, etc. Isaiah uses the phrase, "Holy one of Israel," thirty times. The angels sang, "Holy, Holy, Holy" (Isaiah 6:1-3). Of the many things that were stressed in Israel's relationship to Jehovah, none was stressed any more than holiness or separation.

In the New Testament, we learn that God's children are to be

---

[1] Also, read Acts 3:14; I Corinthians 1:30; I Peter 3:18; Philippians 3:9.

partakers of His Holiness, and thereby become holy (set apart) unto the Lord (II Peter 1:3,4; 1 Peter 1:13-15; Psalm 110:3). Christ is to us today what God was to His people in the long ago. He sanctified Himself, that we might be sanctified by His blood. (Read Hebrews 4:14-16; 7:26; John 17:19; Hebrews 10:9,10; Ephesians 5:25-27.)

Jehovah-shalom. This compound name means, "Jehovah is our peace." The word **shalom** means peace; and is found in Judges **6:24,** "There Gideon built an altar unto Jehovah and called it Jehovah-shalom." The word is also translated as **finished** in I Kings **9:25;** as **whole** in Deuteronomy **27:6;** as **full** in Genesis **15:16;** as **well** in Genesis **43:27;** as **pay** in Psalm **50:14;** as **perfect** in I Chronicles **29:19;** I Kings **8:61;** etc. **Shalom** is translated "peace" **170** times in the Old Testament. The basic idea underlying all these translations of **shalom** is that harmony of relationship has been established upon the basis of paying a debt or satisfying a demand. Under the Law of Moses, this significance is seen in the "peace offering" made by Israel unto Jehovah. (Read Leviticus **3.**) The Bible makes it clear in many places that Jehovah is the source of true peace; e.g.: "...The Lord will bless His people with peace" (Psalm **29:11);** "If ye walk in my statutes, and keep my commandments, and do them...I will give you peace..." (Leviticus **3:3,6).** (Read Isaiah **48:18; 66:12;** Ezekiel **33:11;** Numbers **6:24-26;** Isaiah **26:12.)**

Isaiah prophesied of a coming Prince of Peace (Isaiah 9:6). According to New Testament fulfillment, Jesus Christ is the predicted Prince of Peace (Luke 19:42; John 14:27; 16:33; Mark 9:50; etc.). After His resurrection,
Christ said unto His disciples, "Peace be unto you" (John 20:19). Paul makes it clear that Jesus is our peace (Ephesians 2:14; I Corinthians 4:33); and, therefore, we must be peacemakers, too (Matthew 5:9; II Corinthians 13:11; Colossians 3:15; I Thessalonians 5:13; II Timothy 2:22; James 3:18).

Jehovah-rohi. This compound name means, "Jehovah is my

Shepherd." **Ro'eh** means "to lead, pasture or feed a flock as a shepherd." The word is used many times in the Old Testament to describe the work or activity of a shepherd (Genesis 37:2; 47:3,4; I Samuel 17:15). The word is also used figuratively to describe Jehovah's relationship with His people. The Psalmist said, "Jehovah is my Shepherd..." (Psalm 23:1ff). God was the ever-watchful Shepherd over His people (Israel) throughout their history. Even though they strayed away from Him, He would bring them back (Ezekiel 34:11-16).

Jesus is our Shepherd today: "I am the good shepherd, and know my sheep, and am known of mine. As the Father knoweth me, even so know I the Father: and I lay down my life for the sheep" (John 10:14,15). How wonderful to know that Jesus is the Shepherd of our souls, and that we shall not want (Hebrews 2:9-16; 13:20; I Peter 2:25; etc.).

Jehovah-shammah. This compound name means, "Jehovah is there." **Shammah** conveyed the truth to Israel that the presence and glory of God dwelt in their midst. His dwelling there was contingent upon their obedience to His covenant. Jehovah's presence was manifested in the Tabernacle and Temple (Psalm 132:8,13,14; Exodus 40:34-38; II Chronicles 7:1-3). Ezekiel said, "...and the name of the city from that day shall be, The Jehovah- shammah" (or Jehovah is there) (Ezekiel 48:35).

In Christ Jesus we have the full realization of **Jehovah-shammah.** John said, "The Word became flesh and tabernacled among us" (John 1:14). Jesus became "God with us" (Isaiah 7:14). Before His ascension, Christ promised to be with His followers always (Matthew 28:20). This presence is now in Christians as living temples of Jehovah (I Corinthians 3:16; II Corinthians 6:16; Ephesians 2:19-22). It is wonderful to know that we are not left alone.

Jehovah-nissi. This compound name means, "Jehovah is my banner." Today we would say, "Jehovah is my flag." A banner, however, during the Old Testament period was not necessarily a flag. Ancient banners were usually bare poles with ornaments that glittered on top. In other places in the Old Testament, the word for banner is translated pole, ensign, standard, etc.

In Exodus 17, we find Israel complaining at Rephidim about water and food. While they are busy complaining, an even worse enemy comes upon them (worse than hunger and thirst): "Then came Amalek [Amalekites], and fought with Israel in Rephidim" (Exodus 17:8). During the battle God was with Israel as Moses, with Aaron's help, held his hands high in the air (Exodus 17:9-14). After the victory, "Moses built an altar, and called the name of it **Jehovah-nissi:** For he said, Because the Lord hath sworn that the Lord will have war with Amalek from generation to generation" (Exodus 17:15,16). Therefore, when God is on our side, and we are marching under His flag, we cannot fail.

Today as Christians, we must fight the good fight of faith (II Timothy 4:7), and endure hardship as a good soldier of Christ (II Timothy 2:3,4). Our weapons are not carnal, but spiritual (Ephesians 6:11-17). In our warfare, we are assured victory because Jesus is our banner (I John 5:4; Ephesians 1:19-22; Romans 8:31,37; I Corinthians 15:57,58; II Corinthians 2:14).

Jehovah-rophe. This compound name means, "Jehovah heals." The word **rophe** means to cure, to restore, to heal, or physician. It is used in a physical and spiritual sense in the Old Testament, in which it appears over sixty times. This name is first mentioned in Exodus 15:26: "...Give ear to his commandments and keep his statutes, I will put none of these diseases upon thee, which I have brought upon the Egyptians: for I am Jehovah that healeth thee." Therefore, if Israel will continue to obey God's will, He will be their Healer, both physically and spiritually. (Read Numbers 12:13; Jeremiah 30:15; Psalm 103:2,3; Jeremiah 30:26; 8:21,22.)

Jehovah-rophe is fully realized in Jesus Christ, the great Physician (Isaiah 61:1; Luke 4:18,23) and Healer (Matthew 4:23; 11:4,5; 9:12).

Man's greatest disease—sin—now has a cure, because of His death on the cross (John 4:13,14; Revelation 1:5; I Peter 2:24; Luke 4:18). This is the Good News that must be preached to every creature (Matthew 28:18-20; Mark 16:15,16).

Jehovah-kanna. This compound name means, "Jehovah is jealous." The word **kanna,** which is translated "jealous," did not carry the bad concept that is now associated with it. **Kanna** conveyed the idea of "righteous zeal, warmth or passion." Jehovah was zealous for His own glory (Isaiah 9:7; Zechariah 1:14; 8:2), and His covenant people: "For thou shalt worship no other god: for the Lord, whose name is Jealous, is a zealous God (Exodus 34:14; Exodus 20:5; Deuteronomy 5:9; Ezekiel 39:25).

In the New Testament, Jesus Christ is seen showing righteous zeal (John 2:7; cf. Psalm 69:9). As Christians, we are to be zealous (or jealous) for righteousness (Titus 2:14; II Corinthians 9:2).

Jehovah-sabaoth. This compound name means, "Jehovah of hosts." The word "host" is used of heavenly bodies and earthly forces (Genesis 2:1); of the army of Israel (II Samuel 8:16); of the heavenly beings (Psalm 103:21; 148:2; Daniel 4:35). It does not matter where, or what type of hosts may be involved—Jehovah is over all (I Samuel 1:3); He is the King of glory (Psalm 24:10).

Today, Jesus Christ has authority and power over "all things created, that are in heaven, and that are in earth, visible and invisible, whether they be thrones, or dominions, or principalities, or powers: all things were created by Him and for Him" (Colossians 1:16; cf. Matthew 28:18-20). Therefore, the faithful Christian does not have to fear anything or anybody (I John 4:4).

New Testament Names For God:

The three basic words used in the Greek New Testament for God are
(1) **Theos;** (2) **Kurios;** and (3) **Pater.** Greek scholars agree that **Theos**

is the most common name applied to God. **Theos** is used as an equivalent for **El, Elohim,** and **Elyon.** While **Theos** expresses deity, it is also used of the heathen gods. **Kurios** expresses Yahweh (Jehovah) of the Old Testament, as well as **Adonai. Kurios** reveals God as Lord, Ruler, Possessor, and the Mighty One who has legal authority and power. Time and time again in the New Testament, especially in the Epistles, Christ is called Lord **(Kurios)** (James 1:1; Jude 4; I Corinthians 1:3; Matthew 7:21,22; 9:38; Psalm 66:16; cf. Luke 8:39; John 20:28). **Pater** is the Greek name for **father** in the New Testament. As we have pointed out already, God was known to Israel as Father because of the theocratic relationship. Jesus came to reveal the Father. He said, "...he that hath seen me hath seen the Father...I am in the Father, and the Father in me..." (John 14:7,9,10). Vine makes the following interesting comment on **Kurios:**

Whereas the everlasting power and Divinity of God are manifest in creation, His fatherhood in spiritual relationship through faith is the subject of N. T. revelation, and waited for the presence on earth of the Son, Matthew 11:27; John 17:25.

The spiritual relationship is not universal, John 9:42,44 (cf. John 1:12 and Galatians 3:26). [4]

Conclusion

How wonderful and grand are the names of God. It is easy to see why Jehovah did not want His name taken in vain (Exodus 20:7). To do so was to blaspheme and reject the above, and many other, personal qualities of the God Who created heaven and earth. It is equally as wonderful to know that in Christ Jesus, our Savior, we see personified in the flesh the very attributes of God that were revealed by His name in the Old Testament. Truly, if we have seen Him (Christ), we have seen the Father!

QUESTIONS FOR DISCUSSION

1. Why are names important?
2. What name is first used for God in the Old Testament?

3. Discuss why God did not want His name taken in vain.
4. What is the special or covenant name of God?
5. Discuss the compound names of God and their application to Christ.
6. Which name means "Jehovah will provide"? How does this apply today?
7. What does **tsidkenu** mean?
8. Discuss God as Father in the Old Testament.
9. Who is the "Prince of Shalom"?
10. How can God and Christ be our Shepherd? Are there two Shepherds? Explain.
11. What kind of healing is needed today?
12. Discuss "I am that I am."
13. What do **Theos, Kurios,** and **Pater** mean?
14. Discuss "...he that hath seen me hath seen the Father..."

FOOTNOTES

[1]Nathan J. Stone, *Names of God* (Chicago, IL: Moody Press, 1944), pp. 6-7.

[2]Edward Mack, "Names of God" in *International Standard Bible Encyclopedia,* ed. James Orr (Grand Rapids: Wm. B. Eerdman Publishing Company, 1956), 2:1265.

[5]P. B. Fitzwater, *Christian Theology* (Grand Rapids, MI: Wm. B. Eerdman Pub. Co., 1948), p. 77.

[4]W. E. Vine, *An Expository Dictionary of New Testament Words* (Old Tappan, NJ: Fleming H. Revell Co., 1966), Vol. 2, p. 82.

Chapter Four
THE ESSENCE OF GOD
Introduction

Theologians through the years have disagreed among themselves in the usage of **essence** and **attribute,** relative to discussing what God is. From these theologians, two basic classifications seem to emerge: (1) Natural or absolute attributes; and (2) Relative or moral attributes. Some refer to these two divisions as communicable and incommunicable attributes.2 Our purpose in this study is not to get bogged down in a play on words. We will define the word we are using and then proceed from that definition to use it that way in our study. We must, however, remember that the words "essence" and "attributes" are used interchangeably sometimes in the study of God.

In asking the question "What is God?" we are asking a question, according to our definition, relative to the **essence** of God. Essence is defined by Webster as, "An entity; that which makes something what it is." Essence is the Latin word **essentia,** which comes from **essens,** participle of **esse,** and means **to be.** The words substance, nature, and being are synonymous with essence. For example, if we look at a tree and conclude that it is round and tall, we are describing one of the outward characteristics of a tree. If, however, we say that the tree is wood and begin to discuss the substance of wood, we are discussing what underlies or causes the tree to be tall and round—we are talking about the essence of the tree. In dealing with the essence of God, we are dealing with that which underlies all the outward manifestations of God. Essence, therefore, deals with what God is. As we have already pointed out, we want to make it clear in the very beginning that we are making a distinction between essence

---

2 The communicable attributes are those which can be imparted to man; e.g., goodness, love, holiness, etc. The incommunicable are those attributes which cannot be imparted to or possessed by man; e.g., self-sufficiency, boundlessness, omniscience, etc.

and attribute. An attribute, in our usage, is a revealed moral characteristic of Jehovah which is usually described in anthropomorphic language or terms. Essence, in our usage, is the unobservable, natural reality of being, whether material or immaterial, behind the attribute. Benjamin B. Warfield makes a comment worthy of consideration at this point. He said,

We cannot separate the essence and the attributes. Where the essence is, there the attributes are; they are merely the determinants of the essence. And where the attributes are, there the essence is; it is merely the thing, of the kind of which they are the determinants.[2]

Thinkers, philosophers, and theologians through the years have tried to answer the question, "What is God?" Their answers range from "God is Absolute" to "God is only the product of human thought and wishes." The Westminster Catechism defines God in the following way, "God is a Spirit, infinite, eternal, and unchangeable in his being, wisdom, power, holiness, justice, goodness, and truth." As we study the essence and attributes of God, we will find that this definition is in harmony with revealed truth about God. We must point out, however, that this definition is not complete, because it is not possible for finite man to define an Infinite God. True, we can know all that God has revealed about Himself in the Bible and nature; but we must not conclude that this is **all** there is to know about God. Therefore, in our study of the essence of God, we will note the following revealed truths which God deemed sufficient for us to know.

God Is Spirit

The substance or essence of God is spirit, not material. Jesus said, "God is a Spirit: and they that worship him must worship him in spirit and in truth" (John 4:24). It is not possible to illustrate, in the final analysis, a spirit by any known material substance. It is simply that which is unseen, but real. For example, nobody has ever seen the spirit of life within a human body; but we all believe and know that it exists. The substance of spirit, therefore, is immaterial and incorporeal. Christ said, "Behold my hands and my feet, that it is I myself: handle me, and see; for a spirit hath not flesh and bones, as ye see me have" (Luke 24:39).

The Spirit essence of God is one reason, no doubt, why He did not want Israel, or anybody else, to make an image to represent Him. It is not possible to use the material to represent the spiritual (Deuteronomy 4:15-19). How sad it must have been for Moses to come down from the mountain and find Aaron and the golden calf he had made to represent God (Exodus 32).

Several times the invisible nature of God is pointed out in the Bible. Paul said, "For the invisible things of him from the creation of the world are clearly seen, being understood by the things that are made" (Romans 1:20). John said, "No man hath seen God at any time; the only begotten Son, which is in the bosom of the Father, he hath declared him" (John 1:18). God made it very clear that no man could see Him and live (Exodus 33:20). (Read Colossians 1:15; I Timothy 1:17, 6:16.)

The worship of God is commensurate with His Spirit essence. It must be "in spirit and in truth" (John 4:24). Paul said, "What is it then? I will pray with the spirit, and I will pray with the understanding also: I will sing with the spirit, and I will sing with the understanding also" (I Corinthians 14:15). God wants a man to worship Him from the inward heart, not just outward acts, etc.

The Spirit essence of God explains how He can be Omnipresent. The Psalmist said,

Whither shall I go from thy spirit? or whither shall I flee from thy presence? If I ascend up into heaven, thou art there: If I make my bed in hell, behold, thou art there. If I take the wings of the morning, and dwell in the uttermost parts of the sea, even there shall thy hand lead me (Psalm 139:7-10).

While God is spirit, it does not exclude the idea of life. It is difficult for the human mind to comprehend life in an immaterial essence. Many times in the Bible, however, God is called the **living** God. Peter said, "...Thou art the Christ, the Son of the Living God" (Matthew 16:16). Joshua said, "...Hereby you shall know that the living God is among you..." (Joshua 3:10). Paul said, "...ye turned to God from idols to serve the living and true God" (I Thessalonians 1:9). The Psalmist paints a very graphic picture of dead idols in contrast to the living God. He said:

But our God is in the heavens: he hath done whatsoever he hath pleased. Their idols are silver and gold, the work of men's hands. They have mouths, but they speak not: eyes have they, but they see not: They have ears, but they hear not: noses have they, but they smell not: They have hands, but they handle not: feet have they, but they walk not: Neither speak they through their throat. They that make them are like unto them; so is every one that trusteth in them (Psalm 115:3-8).

Jehovah is life, and the source and sustainer of all life!

The Spirit essence has a personality. The personality of God is contrary to idealistic philosophy, which states that God is an impersonal force. To say that God has a personality is not to reduce Him to the level of man.

We know that God is a person because this is revealed to us. It would not be possible to know what spirit is like, apart from Bible teaching and an analogy with our own spirit. Our human spirit is personal; therefore, we can understand the personality of God, The Scripture uses many anthropomorphic phrases and words in describing the personality of God. Notice the four following areas:

A. **God is ascribed human actions:**

1. He knows.
   (Genesis 18:21)
2. He speaks.

7. He answers.
   (Psalm 3:4)
8. He smells.

(Genesis 2:6) (Genesis 8:21)
3. He hears. 9. He tastes.
(Exodus 2:24) (Psalm 11:4,5)
4. He remembers. 10. He sits.
(Genesis 8:1) (Psalm 9:7)
5. He rebukes. 11. He commands.
(Psalm 18:15) (Isaiah 5:6)
6. He walks. 12. He calls.
(Leviticus 26:12) (Romans 4:17)

God is said to have bodily organs:
1. He has a heart. 4. He has arms.
(Genesis 6:6) (Exodus 15:16)
2. He has a countenance. 5. He has eyes.
(Exodus 33:20) (Psalm 11:4)
3. He has hands. 6. He has a nose.
(Exodus 15:12) (Deuteronomy 33:10)

Human works are ascribed to God:
1. Man of war 4. Shepherd
(Exodus 15:3) (Psalm 23:1)
2. Hero 5. Bridegroom
(Psalm 78:65) (Isaiah 61:10)
3. Builder 6. Husbandman
(Hebrews 11:10) (John 15:1)

D. **Human emotions are ascribed to God:**
1. Grief 5. Vengeance
(Psalm 78:40) (Deuteronomy 32:35)
2. Anger 6. Hatred
(Jeremiah 7:18,19) (Deuteronomy 16:22)
3. Joy 7. Love
(Isaiah 62:5) (John 3:16)

4. Wrath		8.	Rejoicing
(Psalm 2:5)			(Isaiah 65:19)

God, as personality, has all-power of self-determination and self-consciousness in the highest degree. God is, **"I am that I am"** (Exodus 3:14). Job, in the long ago, said, "What his soul desireth, even that he doeth" (Job 23:13). When something is caused by external sources or forces, it is rightly called a **thing.** That which has its cause from within itself is a person. Therefore, God is not a **thing** or an **it,** but a person. (Read Isaiah 45:5; I Corinthians 2:10; Romans 9:11; Hebrews 6:17.)

In our discussion of the personality of the essence, we must be careful to note that the **essence** cannot be one person and at the same time be three persons. There is one personal Being, who by self-determination and self- consciousness exists in three distinct personalities in the Godhead. Likewise, each of the three persons in the Godhead has self-determination and self- consciousness.

God Is Boundless:

God's boundlessness refers to His relationship to time, space, matter and whatsoever is beyond that. In simple terms, God is not bound; He has no limits. The infinity or immensity of God is beyond human comprehension. In our limited concept, we might ask, "How big is God?" This question is out of order when applied to God. Big is a relative term that involves a comparison. For example, a dog is big when compared to a mouse, etc. It is not possible to define God in terms of bigness. He simply is not contained in space or comparable to any known object. The following passages teach the boundlessness of God:

But will God indeed dwell on the earth? Behold, the heaven and heaven of heavens cannot contain thee; how much less this house that I have builded? (I Kings 8:27).

...The heaven is my throne, and the earth my footstool... (Isaiah 66:1).

(Read also Psalms 139:7-10, 145:3; Job 11:7-9; Romans 11:33; Acts 7:48,49; Jeremiah 23:23,24; Acts 17:27,28.)

While God is not contained in space, He is omnipresent. God's essence fills the universe, while at the same time He transcends it. This does away with the false concept of God's **parts** being diffused into different parts of the universe. Such a concept takes away from God's immensity. Empedocles, the Greek philosopher, rightly said, "God is a circle whose center is everywhere, and his circumference nowhere."

As we reflect upon the boundlessness of God, we cannot help but to meditate upon these words, "But one in a certain place testified, saying, what is man, that thou art mindful of him? or the son of man, that thou visitest him?" (Hebrews 2:6; cf. Psalm 8:4; 111:5; 115:12). Compared to the immensity of God, how small and insignificant is man. It is overwhelming to know that the boundless God is so mindful of man that He has numbered the hairs of his head, and knows what he shall say before he says it (Matthew 10:30; Psalm 139:2-6). Also, in light of the immensity of God, think of the equality that Christ gave up to come down to earth and die for us on the cross (Philippians 2:5-8). He, whom the heaven and the heaven of the heavens could not contain, came down to be born in the womb of a virgin (Isaiah 7:14; Matthew 1:20-22). Truly, this should cause a man to see God's great love and concern for him!

God Is Eternal:

The eternal essence of God relates to time and space. God is not contained in space, and is without beginning or end. Many attempts have been made to illustrate how "long" eternity is. The use of the word "long" is improper when applied to eternity, because it suggests measure. Eternity is not measurable; neither is it fully comprehensible by the human mind. This is true because we have nothing to compare it with. Our life is lived by the clock in minutes, hours, weeks, days, months, years, etc. God is not limited or contained by time. He established time in eternity for His creation. A seminary professor once said, in trying to define time, "Time is only parenthesis in eternity."

ETERNITY
(Time)
ETERNITY

True, this is a simple definition; but it serves to illustrate, in some small way, that which in the final analysis is unillustratable. Therefore, the best definition of eternal is, "that which is without beginning or end."

Notice the following passages on the eternity of God:

Before the mountains were brought forth, or ever thou hadst formed the earth and the world, even from everlasting to everlasting, thou art God (Psalm 90:2).

But thou art the same, and thy years shall have no end (Psalm 103:27).

For I lift up my hand to the heaven and say, I live for ever (Deuteronomy 32:40).

...I the Lord, the first, and with the last; I am he (Isaiah 41:4).

...I am the first, and the last; and beside me there is no God (Isaiah 44:6; cf. Revelation 1:8,11).

To the only wise God our Saviour, be glory and majesty, dominion and power, both now and ever (Jude 25).

The eternal God is thy refuge, and underneath are the everlasting arms... (Deuteronomy 33:27).

(Read also Isaiah 57:15; 60:15; Ephesians 3:11; I Timothy 1:17; Romans 1:20.)

The eternal God does not view time as we view it. He views all time, from beginning to end, as **now.** "A thousand years in thy sight are but as yesterday when it is past" (Psalm 90:4; Cf. II Peter 3:8; Hebrews 13:8; Revelation 1:4). The eternal I am's relationship to time as the present helps us understand prophecy and the Omniscience of God; e.g., God called Cyrus by name scores of years before he was born (Isaiah 44:28; cf. II Chronicles 36:22). From the creation until the consummation of all things, God views the **total** parenthesis of time; He is not limited or trapped in the parenthesis of time as we are. How marvelous is the eternity of Jehovah!

God Is Self-Sufficient:

The self-sufficiency of God refers to the needs of God. God has no needs beyond Himself. He does not have to go outside of Himself for anything. How contrasting this is to the many, many needs of man, who must constantly go to an external source for help and resources. Paul said, "Not that we are sufficient of ourselves to think anything as of ourselves; but our sufficiency is of God" (II Corinthians 3:5). Of everything in heaven and on earth, etc., Jehovah is the only One who is self-sufficient. All that is, is dependent upon Him (Psalm 37:17; 41:12; 63:8; 51:12; 54:4; 119:116; 145:1; Ephesians 1:11).

God's self-sufficiency stems from His self-existence. The self-sufficiency and self-existence are conveyed in the name Jehovah—**"I am that I am"** (Exodus 3:14). God exists by the necessity of His own being and nature. Therefore, God is the eternal first cause, who Himself is uncaused and non-dependent. God's self-sufficiency gives us the assurance that we can always trust Him. He will always remain the same: "yesterday, today, and forever." James said, "Every good gift and every perfect gift is from above, and cometh down from the Father of lights, with whom is no variableness, neither shadow of turning" (James 1:17). What a comfort to know that the self-sufficient God of eternity is our Father.

God Is Unchangeable:

God's boundless, self-sufficient, eternal, spirit essence is immutable and unchangeable. With Jehovah, there is no decrease or increase, no fluxion or deterioration. He, alone, is the absolute perfect, unchangeable One. Malachi 3:6 says, "For I am the Lord, I change not; therefore ye sons of Jacob are not consumed." The Psalmist said, "But thou art the same, and thy years shall have no end" (Psalm 192:27); "The counsel of the Lord standeth forever" (Psalm 33:11). While it is clear that God cannot change His nature, it is equally as clear that He cannot change His word (Psalm 119:160; Matthew 5:18; John 10:35; 12:48) or His will (Jeremiah 26:13; I Samuel 15:11).

Before we leave our remarks on the unchangeableness of God, we should note that some reject this point because of Genesis 6:6, which states, "It repented Jehovah that he had made man." This attitude of "sorrow" or repentance does not involve any real change in the essence of God. Strong makes a good comment on this objection. He says,

The change in God's treatment of men is described anthropomorphically, as if it were a change in God himself—other passages in close conjunction with the first [Genesis 6:6 JJT] being given to correct any possible [Numbers 23:19 JJT] misapprehension. Threats not fulfilled, as in Jonah 3:4,19, are to be explained by their conditional nature. Hence, God's immutability itself renders it certain that his love will adapt itself to every varying mood and condition of his children...God's immutability is not that of the stone that has no internal experience, but rather that of the column of mercury that rises and falls with every change in the temperature of the surrounding atmosphere.[3]

Therefore, God may will a change, but He cannot change His will. (Read Luke 11:5-10; 18:1-8.)

Conclusion:

After studying the essence of God, no greater conclusion could be made than that which the Psalmist of old asked, "Who is like unto the Lord our God, who dwelleth on high, who humbleth himself to behold the things that are in heaven, and in the earth! He raiseth up the poor out of the dust, and lifteth the needy out of the dunghill, that he may set him with princes, even with princes of his people."

QUESTIONS FOR DISCUSSION

1. Discuss attributes and essence. Why make a distinction?
2. What is meant by "natural and moral attributes"?
3. Can we separate the essence from the attributes? Discuss.
4. How has God been defined by some men?
5. Discuss the difference between what God is and what God does.
6. What is God's substance? Discuss.
7. Discuss the personal attributes of God.
8. How is God boundless? Discuss the term "big."
9. Discuss your views of eternity.
10. What does God have need of?
11. How does God change? Discuss.
12. How do you feel toward the essence of God?
13. Can you think of something that God does not know?
14. Discuss the worship of God in light of His Spirit essence.

FOOTNOTES

[1] *Webster's New World Dictionary* (Nashville, TN: The Southwestern Co., 1967), p. 257.

[2] Benjamin B. Warfield, "Godhead" in *International Standard Bible Encyclopedia,* ed. James Orr (Grand Rapids: Wm. B. Eerdman Publishing Company, 1956), 2:1270.

[3] A. Strong, *Systematic Theology* (Old Tappan, NJ: Fleming H. Revell Co., 1906), p. 254.

Chapter Five
THE TRIUNE GODHEAD
Introduction

This doctrine is covered under the heading of "Trinity" in the field of Theology. The average Bible reader knows, however, that the word "trinity" is not in the Bible. Therefore, if we follow the rule of using Bible language to describe Bible things, we will have to be careful in our use of this word. This is necessary because of the confusion that exists about it, and the improper concepts it sometimes conveys. **Trinity** comes from the Latin **trinus,** which means triple. An example of vagueness is Webster's definition of trinity, which could be interpreted in favor of Tritheism (we will discuss this term later). He says, "A set of three persons or things that form a unit; in Christian theology, the union of the three divine persons (Father, Son, and Holy Ghost) in one Godhead." ' Theologically, we will be safe in using the word if we are careful to define it as the term that shows the distinctions in the One Divine essence of the three personalities— Father, Son, and Spirit. Therefore, in our use of the word "trinity," we are referring to the tri-personality of the One Divine God.

The Bible does not set forth in a systematic way the doctrine of the trinity. As a formulated doctrine, most attribute its formation to Tertullian in the second century. It was issued as a formal decree by the Council of Nicaea (A.D. 325), in opposition to Arianism3 and Sabellianism, the doctrine of three unequal persons in God. The Christians of the first century did not develop or need a systematic doctrine on the trinity. They followed the Scriptures as revealed. It was not until the second century that men started to formulate doctrines deducted from Bible truths about the Godhead.

The doctrine of the "Trinity" has rightly been called a mystery.

---

[3] Many cults today, such as Unitarians and Jehovah's Witnesses, etc., still follow the doctrine of Arius, and view Christ as a created god and the Spirit as only a force.

The existence of three persons in One essence is beyond human comprehension. We must admit, also, that this doctrine is one of the deepest to be found in the Bible; and in the final analysis, it must be accepted by faith. This doctrine is not provable from natural theology or empirical observation. Man would never have known of the trinity of God without revelation from God.

Charles Hodge makes the following good comment on the uniqueness of the Bible doctrine of the trinity:

The doctrine of the Trinity is peculiar to the religion of the Bible. The Triad of the ancient world is only a philosophical statement of the pantheistic theory which underlies all the religions of antiquity. With the Hindus, simple, undeveloped, primal being, without consciousness or attributes, is called Braham. This being, as unfolding itself in the actual world, is Vishnu; as returning into the abyss of unconscious being, it is Shiva. In Buddhism, we find essentially the same ideas, in more dualistic form. Buddhism makes more of a distinction between God, or the spiritual principle of all things, and nature. The soul of man is a part, or an existence-form, of this spiritual essence, whose destiny is that it may be freed from nature and lost in the infinite unknown. In Platonism, also, we find a notional Trinity. Simple being (to'on-GK) has its logos, the complex of its ideas, the reality in all that is phenomenal and changing. In all these systems, whether ancient or modern, there is a Thesis, Antithesis, and Synthesis; the Infinite becomes finite, and the finite returns to the Infinite. It is obvious, therefore, that these trinitarian formulas have no analogy with the Scriptural doctrine of the Trinity, and serve neither to explain nor confirm it.[2]

Tritheism

It should be made clear in the very beginning of our study that the trinity of God is not Tritheism. Tritheism denies the unity of three equal persons in the essence of God and holds to three distinct Gods. When the Tritheist speaks of unity, he is referring only to unity of purpose, aim, and endeavor. The trinity of the Godhead is not a divine partnership in which each personality is a distinct essence, apart from the agreed unity. The unity exists within the One eternal essence.

The Tritheist sect first appeared in the sixth century, and taught that the Father, Son, and Spirit were three co-equal, distinct Beings, united by one common will and purpose. Cyril of Jerusalem attributes the origin of Tritheism in its broadest form to Marcion, and Hilary associates it with the heresy of Photinus. [3]

BerkhoPs statement on the doctrine of the Trinity helps to clarify in greater detail our opposition to Tritheism:

In the One Divine essence there are three persons or individual subsistences, Father, Son, and Holy Spirit...Every person is a distinct and separate individual, in whom human nature is individualized. But in God there are no three individuals alongside of, and separate from, one another, but only personal self-distinctions within Divine essence, which is not only generically, but numerically, one.

The total essence of God belongs equally to each of the three persons. Paul taught that Jesus left this equality to come down and live among men (Philippians 2:5-8). Again let us note Berkhof's comments on this point of equality:

Essence is not divided among three, but wholly in each one of the persons, so that they have a numerical unity of essence. The divine nature is distinguished from the human nature in that it can subsist **wholly** and indivisibly in more than one person. While three persons among men have only a **specific** unity of nature or essence, that is, share in the same kind of nature or essence, the persons in the Godhead have a **numerical** unity of essence, that is, possess the identical essence...It follows that the divine essence is not an independent existence alongside of the three persons. If it did, that would lead into tetratheism.[5] (Read Colossians 2:9.)

Therefore, the unity of God is contrary to Tritheism (three gods), and polytheism (many gods). God's unity is the doctrine of Monotheism (One Supreme Being), which eliminates all other gods, but is inclusive of three persons within the Godhead.

Illustrating the Trinity

There have been many attempts by man to illustrate the Trinity. As we have already noted, it is not possible for finite man to illustrate an Infinite God. This is especially true with regard to the doctrine of God's trinity of personalities within the One essence. Herman Bavinck discusses some of the attempts made by man to illustrate the Trinity, plus the impossibility of such attempts:

(1) Illustrations taken from Scripture: three patriarchs, three divisions of the tabernacle, three beloved disciples, three witnesses, etc.
(2) Analogies taken from the realm of heathendom: the Trimurti of the Indians, etc.
(3) Similitudes in nature: fountain, rivulet, and stream; root, trunk, and branches, etc.
(4) Resemblances in the sphere of logic, grammar: first, second, and third person, etc.
(5) Approximations in the processes of our minds: memory, understanding, and will, etc.
(6) Various philosophical reconstructions of the doctrine of the Trinity have been attempted.
(7) Criticism: the analogies taken from the realm of heathendom are without any value; as to the illustrations in general: in all of them, we have a certain trinity but no tripersonality in unity of substance; not any of these analogies nor all of them, together can prove the Divine Trinity; for that doctrine we are dependent wholly on Scripture. Nevertheless, these illustrations serve to prove that belief in the Divine Trinity is not absurd or unreasonable.[6]

Therefore, it is not possible, from the human standpoint, to illustrate the Trinity.4 Any attempt to do so will be inadequate, and thus will take away from this great truth. In the following Scriptures, both in the Old and New Testaments, we shall see the truth about the trinity of the Godhead. While we may not fully comprehend it, let us, however, fully believe it.

Plurality in the Old Testament

The Old Testament stresses the unity of God, while at the same time many intimations occur concerning a plurality in the Godhead. The Old Testament does not reveal that this plurality is triune (three in one). As we have already noted, plural nouns and pronouns with singular verbs are applied to God:

In the beginning God [Elohim, plural] created the heavens and the earth (Genesis 1:1).

And God [Elohim] said, Behold, the man is become as one of **us...** (Genesis 3:22).

Come, let us go down, and there confound their language... (Genesis 11:7, cf. Verse 8).

Hear, O Israel: Jehovah [singular] our God [Elohim, plural] is one Jehovah [singular] (Deuteronomy 6:4; here the plural is called one).

Another interesting passage on plurality in the Old Testament is Ecclesiastes 12:1. It says, "Remember also thy Creator in the days of thy youth..." The Hebrew word for Creator, in this passage, is plural. This passage, however, agrees with the statement in Genesis one, where God is revealed as Elohim (plural). It says, "Let **us** [plural] make man in **our** [plural] image..." (verse 26). Isaiah also said, "For thy Maker [plural] is thy husband [plural] (Isaiah 54:3).

Psalm 110:1 says, "Jehovah saith unto my Lord, Sit thou at my right hand." The word **Lord** in this verse is **Adonai,** a title never given

---

4 Even the word "person" does not fully convey the Biblical truth of persons in the Godhead. Although this word, more nearly than any other single word (anthropomorphic), expresses the conception which the Scriptures give us of the relation between the Father, Son, and Spirit, it is not itself used in this connection in Scripture, and we employ it in a qualified sense, not in the ordinary sense in which we apply the word "person" to Peter, Paul, and John.[7]

to any but the true God. Peter applied this verse to Christ in Acts 2:34,35. Therefore, we have inner-communication in the Godhead expressed in this verse (cf. Hebrews 1:13), which is another point in favor of plurality.

Before we leave the Old Testament, it would be good to point out that Isaiah prophesied of a child to be born, who was to be called Immanuel, which means God with us; i.e., God in our nature (or flesh) (Isaiah 7:14). He was also to be called, "Wonderful, Counselor, Mighty God, Everlasting Father, Prince of Peace" (Isaiah 9:6). Christ was Immanuel (Matthew 1:21-23).

Plurality in the New Testament

The plurality that was a numerical mystery in the Old Testament has been revealed as triune in the New Testament. Paul states that Jesus left His equality in the Godhead to come down and dwell in a tabernacle of flesh (Philippians 2:5-8). John argues that the Logos (Christ) existed in the beginning (John 1:1-14). Let us notice the following Scriptural proofs for coequality in the One Divine essence:

The Father, Son, and Holy Spirit are eternal:

(a) Father: "I am the first, and I am the last" (Isaiah 44:6); the everlasting God (Romans 16:26).
(b) Son: "I am the first and the last" (Revelation 1:17, cf. Micah 5:2).
(c) **Holy Spirit:** "...Who through the eternal Spirit offered himself..." (Hebrews 9:14).

The Father, Son, and Holy Spirit are recognized as God:

(a) **Father:** "Elect according to the foreknowledge of God the Father..." (I Peter 1:2).
(b) **Son:** "But of the Son he saith, Thy throne, O God, is forever and ever..." (Hebrews 1:8, cf. John 1:1; Romans 9:5; Titus 2:13).
(c) **Holy Spirit:** "...Why hath Satan filled thy heart to lie to the Holy Spirit...thou hast not lied to men, but unto God" (Acts 5:3,4). (Note: Spirit and God are used interchangeably.)

The Father, Son, and Holy Spirit have created:

(a) **Father:** "...the Father, of whom are all things..." (II Corinthians 8:6); "...Jehovah...hath made us..." (Psalm 100:3).
(b) **Son:** "For in him were all things created..." (Colossians **1:16,** cf. John **1:1-3).**
(c) **Holy Spirit:** "The Spirit of God hath made me, and the breath of the Almighty giveth me life" (Job 33:4, cf. Isaiah 40:13; Genesis 1:2,26).

The Father, Son, and Holy Spirit are said to be omnipresent:
(a) **Father:** "Do I not fill the earth: saith the Lord" (Jeremiah 23:24).
(b) **Son:** "...Lo, I am with you always..." (Matthew 28:20).
(c) **Holy Spirit:** "Whither shall I go from thy Spirit?" (Psalm 139:7).

The three persons are mentioned together, yet separate, in the following passages:
(1) And Jesus, when he was baptized...he saw the Spirit of God descending as a dove...and lo, a voice out of the heavens, saying, This is my beloved Son, in whom I am well pleased (Matthew 3:16,17).
(2) Go ye therefore, and make disciples of all the nations, baptizing them in the name of the Father and of the Son and of the Holy Spirit (Matthew 28:19).
(3) The grace of the Lord Jesus Christ, and the love of God, and the communion of the Holy Spirit, be with you all (II Corinthians 13:14).

Praying in the Holy Spirit, keep yourselves in the love of God, looking for the mercy of our Lord Jesus Christ unto eternal life (Jude 20, 21).

Conclusion

While we cannot fully comprehend the triune nature of Deity, we must accept the ample Biblical proofs of its truthfulness. The Bible makes it clear that there is only One, Perfect, Eternal, Divine essence, who alone is the Creator and Sustainer of the universe. In this Divine essence, there are three equal Persons who are called God and who possess Divine attributes. There is also a recognized order among the three Persons which does not take away from Their equality. We must be careful to always view the passages in the Gospels that refer to Christ's subjection to the Father, and His statement that "the Father is greater than I" (John 14:28), as being qualified by the voluntary subjection of the Son while tabernacled in the flesh (Philip- pians 2:5-8). It is overwhelming to see how far God has gone in His effort to redeem fallen man. Equally as sad is man's effort to reduce Christ and the Holy Spirit to the position of a demigod.

Again, our responsibility is not to rationalize or illustrate this great truth, but to accept it by faith as revealed in the Scriptures. Many of the points that were only touched in this chapter, concerning the Divinity of Christ and the Holy Spirit, will be dealt with in greater detail in chapters 8-13.

DISCUSSION QUESTIONS

1. How could the word "trinity" convey the wrong idea?
2. In what sense is the doctrine of the Trinity called a mystery?
3. How does the Biblical doctrine of the triune God differ from heathen trinitarianism? Discuss.
4. Why is revelation (Bible) necessary in order to understand the triune nature of the One God?
5. What is Tritheism?
6. **True or False:** God is a composite of three separate persons formed into a union. **True or False:** Each has a separate essence.
7. How does Monotheism differ from Tritheism and Polytheism?
8. Can we properly illustrate the triune Godhead by comparing Deity to the unity of a human family (i.e., father, mother, and children are one, yet three separate beings)?
9. Discuss "one + one + one = ONE."
10. _____ "Let _____ make man in _____ image..."
11. Where is the Father called God? Where is the Son called God?

Where is the Holy Spirit called God? Give some passages.
12. Discuss the subjection of Jesus to the Father.
13. What is a demigod?
14. How must we finally accept the unity of God doctrine?
15. **True or False:** There is One Divine essence, manifested in three equal Persons, and each of these possess the total Divine essence.
16. Discuss life and the human spirit from the mystery standpoint. How does each person possess the spirit of life? How many spirits of life are there? Has anybody seen the spirit of life?

FOOTNOTES

[1]*Webster's New World Dictionary* (Nashville, TN: The Southwestern Co., 1967), p. 792.

[2]Charles Hodge, *Systematic Theology* (Grand Rapids, MI: Wm. B. Eerd- man Pub. Co., reprint 1970), Vol. 1, p. 442.

[3]John McClintock and James Strong, "Tritheists," *Cyclopedia of Biblical, Theological, and Ecclesiastical Literature* (Grand Rapids, MI: Baker Book House, 1881, reprint 1970), Vol. X-SU-Z, p. 558.

"L. Berkhof, *Systematic Theology* (Grand Rapids, MI: Wm. B. Eerdman Pub. Co., 1968), p. 87.

[5]Ibid., p. 88.

"Herman Bavinck, *The Doctrine of God,* translated and edited by William Hendriksen, (Grand Rapids, MI: Wm. B. Eerdman Pub. Co., 1951), pp. 321-322.

Augustus H. Strong, *Systematic Theology* (Old Tappan, NJ: Fleming H. Revell Co., 1907, reprint 1969), p. 330.

[8]Edward Bickersteth, *The Trinity* (Grand Rapids, MI: Sovereign Grace Publishers, 1971 reprint), p. 84.

Chapter Six
ATTRIBUTES OF GOD (1)

Introduction:
As we have noticed several times in our study, it is very difficult for finite man to describe the Infinite God. We have this problem again as we use the word "attribute" to describe some of God's manifestations to His creation. This word, basically, conveys the idea of adding or assigning something to one. Therefore, it may give the impression that something is being added to the Divine Being. We want to be very clear not to use the word in this sense. Thus, it is necessary to define our term.

Strong defines "attribute" as follows:

The attributes of God are those distinguishing characteristics of the divine nature which are inseparable from the idea of God which constitutes the basis and ground for his various manifestations to his creatures.[1]

Fitzwater, in commenting on the word "attribute," says, "By attribute is meant the quality inherent in the essence of a being or thing. When applied to God, attributes mean the essential qualities inherent in the divine nature. Attribute means more than a characteristic, for a characteristic may be either inherent or acquired. An attribute of God, therefore, means the quality which is essentially an expression of the very being of God. Therefore, the attributes of God are more than mere names or separate parts of a composite God. When we have listed all the attributes, which is not possible, we do not have **all** God is.

Relationship of Attributes to Essence:
In our study of the attributes of God, we are making a distinction between essence and attributes in the following ways:

(1)   Essence is what God is (natural "attributes"); and

(2) Attributes describe what God does in relation to man (moral "attributes").

Admittedly, there is an interchanging of words as we discuss the essence and attributes of God. Again, our problem is one of clarity. Hodge makes a worthy comment at this point. He says:

"It is evident that this question of the relation of the divine attributes to the divine essence merges itself into the general question of the relation between attributes and substance. It is evident that this is a subject about which one man knows just as much as another...[3]

Strong makes the following four points which will help clarify the relation of attributes to the essence:

(1) **The attributes have an objective existence.** They are not mere names for human conceptions of God—conceptions which have their only ground in the imperfection of the finite mind. They are qualities objectively distinguishable from the divine essence and from each other.

(2) **The attributes inhere in the divine essence.** They are not separate existences. They are attributes of God...We cannot conceive of attributes except as belonging to an underlying essence which furnishes their ground of unity. In representing God as a compound of attributes, realism endangers the living unity of the Godhead.

(3) **The attributes belong to the divine essence as such.** They are to be distinguished from those other powers or relations which do not appertain to the divine essence universally. The personal distinctions **(proprietates)** in the nature of the one God are not to be denominated attributes; for each of these personal distinctions belongs not to the divine essence as such and universally, but only to the particular person of the Trinity who bears its name; while on the contrary, all of the attributes belong to each of the persons.

(4) **The attributes manifest the divine essence.** The essence is revealed only through the attributes. Apart from its attributes, it is unknown and unknowable.[4]

God does what He does because of Who He is. Thus, the activities of God are determined by His essence; these activities are manifested by attributes toward the creation or universe. The attributes are sometimes referred to as "natural attributes" (we used the word **essence** to make this distinction), which belong to Him alone. The attributes which we shall discuss in this lesson are called "moral attributes" by some, because they describe His moral qualities. These moral attributes can belong to the child of God in a limited or changing sense. With God, they are absolute and unchanging; He has them to an infinite degree. Therefore, we have the assurance that our Father will remain eternally the same in His essence (natural) and attributes (moral).

Holiness of God:

The holiness of God is one of the most frequent attributes made known by Jehovah to His people in the Old Testament. The word **holy** basically means separate, separation, or transcendency. Time after time, in the Scriptures, God is called "The Holy One." This expression occurs about thirty times in the book of Isaiah alone (e.g., 5:16; 6:1-5). He alone possesses **all** holiness because of His perfect moral excellency. Moses and all the children of Israel sang, "Who is like thee, O Jehovah, among the gods? Who is like thee, glorious in holiness..." (Exodus 15:11). John wrote, "Who shall not fear, O Lord, and glorify thy name? for thou only art holy..." (Revelation 15:4). The Psalmist said, "Exalt ye Jehovah our God, and worship at his holy hill; for Jehovah our God is holy" (Psalm 99:9); "Once have I sworn by holiness: I will not lie unto David" (Psalm 89:35). Amos said, "The Lord Jehovah hath sworn by his holiness..." (Amos 4:2). John said, "...God is light, and in him is no darkness at all" (I John 1:5). The absence of darkness shows Jehovah's perfect holiness. (Read Matthew 5:14-16.)

The word **holy** is also used to describe many things that relate to Jehovah:5

But Jehovah is in his holy temple... (Habakkuk 2:20).

...Separate unto you between the holy place and the most holy place (Exodus 26:33).

...the place whereon thou standest is holy ground (Exodus 3:5).

...They brought the ark of Jehovah...and all the holy vessels... (I Kings 8:4).

Remember the Sabbath day, to keep it holy (Exodus 20:8).

All of these things were holy because they were separated unto His service, etc.

The word **holy** is applied to men:

...Ye are holy unto Jehovah... (Ezra 8:28).

...Behold now, I perceive that this is a holy man of God... (I Kings 4:9).

And ye shall be unto me a kingdom of priests, and a holy nation... (Exodus 19:6).

In the New Testament, each member of the Godhead is referred to as holy:

...Holy Father, keep them in thy name which thou hast given me... (John 17:11).

But ye denied the Holy and Righteous One, and asked for a murderer to be granted unto you (Acts 3:14).

And the disciples were Filled with joy and with the Holy Spirit (Acts 13:52, Cf. Acts 2:38; 5:32).

The New Testament makes it clear that God's children must be holy or separated from the world and sin:

But like as he who called you is holy, be ye yourselves also holy in all manner of living (I Peter 1:15).

Even as he chose us in him before the foundation of the world, that we should be holy and without blemish before him in love

---

5 One writer gives 80 ways the word "holy" is used in the Bible.

(Ephesians 1:4).

But ye are an elect race, a royal priesthood, a holy nation, a people for God's own possession, that ye may show forth the excellencies of him who called you out of darkness into his marvellous light (I Peter 2:9).

Because Jehovah is high and holy, He hates sin. The Proverb writer says, "The thoughts of the wicked are an abomination to the Lord" (Proverbs 15:26); "The froward is an abomination to the Lord" (Proverbs 3:32). Habakkuk declared, "O Jehovah...Thou that art of purer eyes than to behold evil, and thou canst not look on perverseness..." (Habakkuk 1:12,13). This is why sin separates men from the holy God of heaven (Isaiah 59:1,2). Therefore, we are told, "the wages of sin is death; but the free gift of God is eternal life in Christ Jesus our Lord" (Romans 6:23). God's holiness, however, did not cause Him to remain aloof from sinful man. Many times in the Old Testament we see Jehovah involved in the affairs of Israel (Isaiah 57:15-21). God's holiness is manifested in the death of Christ on the cross. Because of His Infinite holiness, God provided the perfect atonement for sin, by sacrificing His only Begotten Son (John 1:29; Matthew 26:28; Revelation 1:5). Thus, if a man would be holy today, he must come by way of the cross (Galatians 2:20).

The holiness of God should cause us to respect Him in our every action and word. There are some today who treat God as a "buddy" or as an "old man." They address him, even in prayer, in blasphemous language. May we, as Isaiah, constantly see God "high and lifted up" (Isaiah 6:1). May we never be charged with the charge Jehovah brought against His people in the long ago. He said, "Thou thoughtest that I was altogether as thyself' (Psalm 50:21); then, "exalt ye the Lord our God and worship at His footstool; He is holy" (Psalm 99:5).

God's Love:

The love of God is misunderstood by many today. Many people, in thinking about or discussing God's love, have a tendency to equate it with the love of man for his fellow man, etc. Thus, God's love is viewed as indulgent, changeable, sentimental, emotional, etc. Those who hold such views usually believe that God will permit and overlook manys things which He has forbidden. One man said, "God will not send a person to hell, because He is a God of love." This person failed to understand God's love and its relationship to His divine justice.

In studying the love of God, we are studying an attribute that rightly belongs under the heading of God's essence; but, because we are viewing His love in relation to man, we shall study it under the heading of attribute (again, a weakness of man's trying to understand God). "Love is the most characteristic attribute of fatherhood. It is the abstract term that most fully expresses the concrete character of God as Father."

John, the apostle of love, writes, "He that loveth not knoweth not God; for God is love" (I John 4:8). All of the attributes of God manifested toward man are directed by His love. God's love is not influenced, as man's is, by who or what we are. Paul wrote, "God commendeth His love toward us, in that, while we were yet sinners, Christ died for us" (Romans 5:8). This love has no boundaries or restrictions; it is universal toward all men (John 3:16). While God hates sin, His divine love for the sinner motivated Him to send His only Begotten Son to die on the cross for our redemption (cf. Ephesians 2:4; II Thessalonians 2:16; Titus 3:4; 1 John 4:9,10). Jesus died for us because he loved us (Revelation 1:5).

The love of God is mentioned many times in the Old Testament:
1. Because he loved thy father, therefore he chose their seed after them (Deuteronomy 4:37, cf. 9:39).
2. The Lord loveth the righteous (Psalm 146:8).
3. I have loved thee with an everlasting love: therefore will I give men for thee, and people for thy life (Jeremiah 31:3).

4. I have loved you, saith the Lord (Jeremiah 31:3).

Time and time again in the Old Testament, God's love is exemplified in His longsuffering toward Israel. Only an Infinite God could continue to love a people who had perpetually rejected Him by turning to idols.

God has always desired for man to love Him. This is seen in the divine command from God: "And thou shalt love the Lord thy God with all thy heart, and with all thy soul, and with all thy mind, and with all thy strength: this is the first commandment" (Mark 12:30). Love for God, as some seem to think, is not optional, but is necessary if one is to be blessed by the Heavenly Father.

Today, our relationship with God is based upon love. Jesus said, "If ye love me, keep my commandments. He that hath my commandments and keepeth them, he it is that loveth me: and he that loveth me shall be loved of my Father, and I will love him..." (John 14:15,16). If one loves Jesus, he will repent of his sins (Luke 13:3); confess Christ as Lord (Matthew 10:32,33); be baptized for the remission of sins (Mark 16:15,16); and live a faithful life unto death (Revelation 2:10). Therefore, Paul could say, "If any man love not the Lord Jesus Christ, let him be anathema" (I Corinthians 16:22).

Not only must we love God, but the Bible makes it very clear that we must love all others:

(1) We must love our enemies (Matthew 5:43-48).

(2) We must love one another (I John 4:11).

(3) We must love the brethren in the church (I Peter 1:22; I John 3:14).

(4) We must love our neighbor (Matthew 19:19).

(5) Husbands and wives must love each other (Ephesians 5:22,23; I Peter 3:1-6).

(6) We must love ourselves (Matthew 19:19).

Therefore, "Love is of God; and everyone that loveth is begottenof God, and knoweth God. He that loveth not knoweth not God; "for

God is love" (I John 4:7,8). "We love Him, because He first loved us" (I John 4:19).

We conclude our thoughts on love by listing Pink's seven points on God's love:

1,The love of God is uninfluenced (Deuteronomy 7:7,8; II Timothy 1:9).
2. It is eternal (Jeremiah 31:3).
3.It is sovereign (Romans 9:19; Ephesians 1:4,5).
4.It is infinite (Ephesians 2:4; John 3:16).
5.It is immutable (James 1:17-19; Romans 8:35-39).
6.It is holy (I John 1:5; Hebrews 12:6; Romans 5:21).
7.It is gracious (John 3:16; Romans 8:32-39).

May our prayer be: Lord, please help me to love thee, and others, more! Read I Corinthians, chapter 13, for a description of the love we should possess. To see love personified, study the life of Jesus.

Goodness of God:

Goodness within man, because of sin and weakness, fluctuates from time to time. It may be said of man that he is trying to become good and remain good. This, however, is not true with regard to God's goodness. Only God is perfect in His goodness. The Psalmist said, "The goodness of God endures continually" (Psalm 52:1); "Good and upright is Jehovah: Therefore will he instruct sinners in the way" (Psalm 25:8).

When we refer to the goodness of God, we are referring to the perfection of His nature. Pink makes a good observation on the goodness of God, in a quote from Monton. He says,

"He is originally good, good of Himself, which nothing else is; for all creatures are good only by participation and communication with God. He is essentially good; not only good, but goodness itself...He is infinitely good; the creature's good is but a drop, but in God there is an infinite ocean or gathering together of good. He is eternally and immutably good, for He cannot be less good than He is; as there can be no addition made to Him, so no subtraction from Him."

Jesus affirmed the goodness of God when He said, "...Why callest thou me good? there is none good but one, that is, God" (Mark 10:18; Luke 18:18; Matthew 19:16). Charnock makes the following comment on this verse:

Some think that Christ hereby would draw him to an acknowledgment of him as God: You acknowledge me good, how come you salute me with so great a title, since you do not afford it to your greatest doctors? Lightfoot **in loc.** observes that the title of **Rabbi bone** is not in all the Talmud. You must own me to be God, since you own me to be good, goodness being a title only due and properly belonging to the Supreme Being...The Arians used this place to back their denying the deity of Christ; because, say they, he did not acknowledge himself God. But he doth not here deny His deity, but reproves him for calling him good, when he had not yet confessed him to be more than a man. 8

Commensurate with His goodness, everything that Jehovah does is good; likewise His goodness is manifested toward man. Notice God's goodness as seen in:

(1) His creation (Genesis 1:30-31).
(2) His providential care of His creation (Genesis 8:22).
(3) His protection of the righteous (Genesis 7:1-9:29).
(4) His preservation of Israel (Exodus 11:3; 14:19-21; Nehemiah 9:15; Psalm 78:15-20).
(5) His permitting sinners to repent (Romans 2:4).
(6) His answering prayer (James 1:3-8).
(7) His providing a Savior for the lost (John 3:16).
(8) His providing the Scriptures as a rule to guide and direct us (John 12:48; Mark 13:31).
(9) His longsuffering (1 Peter 3:20; II Peter 3:9,15).
(10) His helping in time of temptation (I Corinthians 10:13; James 1:1-7).

(11) His extension of His goodness toward all (Matthew 5:45; Psalm 145:9; Luke 6:35).

Since God is perfect in His goodness, we would do well to heed the words of the Psalmist when he said, "O that men would praise the Lord for His goodness, and for His wonderful works to the children of men" (Psalm 107:8). Nahum, the prophet, said, "The Lord is good, a stronghold in the day of trouble, and He knoweth them that trust in Him" (Nahum 1:7). As children of our Heavenly Father, may we try to be good toward our fellow man—even our enemies. Paul said, "Be not overcome of evil, but overcome evil with good" (Romans 12:21). Spurgeon is reported to have said,

When others behave badly to us, it should only stir us up the more heartily to give thanks unto the Lord, because **He** is good; and when we ourselves are conscious that we are far from being good, we should only the more reverently bless Him that He is good. We must never tolerate an instance of unbelief as to the goodness of the Lord; whatever else may be questioned, this is absolutely certain, that Jehovah is good."

Therefore, "Oh give thanks unto Jehovah; for he is good; for his lovingkindness endureth forever" (Psalm 107:lff).

Conclusion:

Truly, the holiness, love, and goodness of God is perfect. As His children, with His help, let us strive for more holiness, love, and goodness, so that men may see our lives and glorify our Father which is in heaven; also, may we continue to study and learn of the depths of these wonderful attributes as the years come and go.

QUESTIONS FOR DISCUSSION

1. _____ " _____ is very _____ man to _____ the _____ _____ _____ ." Why is this true?

2. **True or False:** Attributes are mere names of composite parts of

God. Discuss.

3. How do attributes differ from the essence?
4. "Essence_____what God_____
5. "Attributes _____ what God _____ in _____
   To_____"
6. Define Holy:_____
7. Other than God, are other persons and things referred to as holy? Why? How?
8. What do John 17:11; Acts 3:15; 13:52, prove?
9. Define love:
10. How is God's love misunderstood?
11. Who does God love?
12. How does God love? Discuss.
13. Define the term goodness:
14. "The_____ of _____ endureth_____"
15. Discuss man's goodness:
16. Discuss how God's goodness is manifested.

FOOTNOTES

[1] A. Strong, *Systematic Theology* (Grand Rapids, MI: Wm. B. Eerdman Pub. Co.), p. 244.

[2] P. B. Fitzwater, *Christian Theology* (Grand Rapids, MI: Wm. B. Eerdman Pub. Co., 1948), p. 81.

[3] Charles Hodge, *Systematic Theology* (Grand Rapids, MI: Wm. B. Eerdman Pub. Co.), p. 371.

[4] Strong, pp. 244-246.

[5] T. Rees, "God" in *International Standard Bible Encyclopedia*, ed. James Orr (Grand Rapids: Wm. B. Eerdman Publishing Company, 1956), 2:1263.

[6] Arthur W. Pink, *The Attributes of God* (Swengel, PA: Reiner Pub., 1966 printing), pp. 70-73.

[7] Ibid., p. 52.

[8]Stephen Charnock, *The Existence and Attributes of God* (Grand Rapids, MI: Sovereign Grace Publishers, 1971 reprint), pp. 533-534.

Chapter Seven
ATTRIBUTES OF GOD (2)
Introduction:

In the last lesson on the attributes of God, we studied the holiness, love, and goodness of God. In this second lesson on the attributes of God, we will study the truthfulness, faithfulness, patience, justice, wrath, grace, and mercy of Jehovah.

The Truthfulness of God

Lying has been called the **common** sin of the day. Many believe that lying is the easiest sin for a person to commit. In a recent article, one writer stated that the average person tells approximately seventeen lies each day. The writer illustrated this by referring to such things as failing to answer the phone. He stated that by not answering the phone, you send a lie to the calling party; by not answering the phone, you are saying, "I am not at home." Another illustration of lying was the making of an appointment at a certain hour, and then not keeping it on the exact minute, etc. It is obvious that lying abounds in the world today. You find it in every area of life; i.e., social, political, business, religious, literary, journalism, etc. America, like Ephraim of old, is compassing God with lies (Hosea 11:12).

> How false are men, both in their heads and hearts!
> And their falsehood in all trades and arts.
> Lawyers deceive their clients by false law;
> Priests, by false gods, keep all the world in awe.
> For their false tongues such flattering knaves are raised,
> For their false wit scribbles by fools are praised.
>
> —John Crown

Society depends upon truth; it cannot hold together without it. Man must be able to have confidence in his fellow man if it is to survive. Therefore, as never before, there is a real need for stressing truthfulness. In the midst of a society that is geared to lying, it is wonderful to know that there is One to Whom we can turn and always find truthfulness. This One is God!

The truthfulness of God is His perfect knowledge of all truth and His never contradicting that truth. Jehovah is the source of truth; anything that contradicts His nature is untrue. The Psalmist said, "Happy is he that hath the God of Jacob for his help, Whose hope is in Jehovah his God: Who keepeth truth for ever" (Psalm 146:5,6). Jehovah, in His holiness, is never led into falsehood. Balaam, in presenting God's will to Balak, said, "God is not a man, that he should lie..." (Numbers 23:19).

In contrast to the truthfulness of God, Satan, our adversary, is pictured as a liar. Jesus said,

Ye are of your father the devil, and the lusts of your father it is your will to do. He was a murderer from the beginning and standeth not in the truth, because there is no truth in him. When he speaketh a lie, he speaketh of his own: for he is a liar, and the father thereof (John 8:44).

Therefore, those who lie are of the devil. In Acts 5:3, we have a good example of Satan encouraging people to lie. Therefore, only a foolish man will lie!

God has demonstrated His truthfulness time and time again. Isaiah said, "...I will praise thy name; for thou hast done wonderful things, even counsels of old, in faithfulness and truth" (Isaiah 25:1). God has exemplified His truthfulness in some of the following ways:

(1) To Adam and Eve (Genesis 2:16,17; cf. 3:16-24).
(2) To Noah (Genesis 7-9).
(3) To Abraham (Genesis 24:27).
(4) To Jacob (Genesis 32:10).
(5) To Israel (Psalm 98:3; Exodus 23:23-31; Leviticus 26:3-13; Joshua 21:43-45).
(6) In sending a Savior (Genesis 3:15; cf. Galatians 4:4; John 1:29).
(7) In keeping all of His promises (Psalm 77:20; II Samuel 7:11; Exodus 34:7; cf. Psalm 65:3).

(8) In providing temporal blessings (Leviticus 26:6; Proverbs 3:10; Matthew 6:25-34).

(9) In bruising Satan (Genesis 3:15; Romans 16:20; Revelation 12:9).

(10) In making a new covenant (Jeremiah 31:31 ff; cf. Hebrews 8, The Hebrew writer said,

"Wherein God being minded to show more abundantly unto the heirs of the promise the immutability of his counsel, interposed with an oath; that by two immutable things, in which it is impossible for God to lie, we have a strong encouragement, who have fled for refuge to lay hold of the hope set before us" (Hebrews 6:17,18).

Therefore, because of His integrity and oath, God kept His promise to Abraham. We, likewise, have the same assurance that God's truthfulness will remain the same toward us.

Since God is truthful and the source of truth, we have the assurance of knowing the truth in religious matters. Men through the years have constantly asked the question that Pilate asked: "What is truth?" (John 18:38). Men have answered this question in various ways:

(1) Truth is relative (may vary from person to person).

(2) Truth is pragmatic (anything that works or satisfies).

(3) Truth is unattainable.

(4) Truth is consistency with facts.

(5) Truth is systematic coherence (if it relates to the completeness of the whole).

While the philosopher bogs down in epistemological nonsense, Jesus says, "And ye shall know the truth, and the truth shall make you free" (John 8:32; read John 1:17). Our quest for religious truth ends with God's word: "Sanctify them in the truth: thy word is truth" (John 17:17). In God's word, and only in God's word, we learn the truth about some of the following things:

(1) Where we came from (Genesis 1:26,27; Matthew 19:4-6).

(2) Why we are here (I Corinthians 6:20; Romans 15:6).

(3) Where we are going (Hebrews 9:27; Romans 14:10).
(4) Whether or not we are saved (I John 5:13; John 20:30,31).
(5) The consequences of sin (Romans 6:23; Isaiah 59:1,2).
(6) How to become a Christian (John 8:24; Luke 13:3; Matthew 10:32,33; Mark 16:16; Revelation 2:10).
(7) How to live a Christian life (II Peter 1:3).

All of this, and much more, is made possible because of God's truthfulness in sending His Son, Who is the truth (John 14:6), to suffer and die on the cross. As children of the truthful heavenly Father, let us strive to be truthful, also, in all things (Colossians 3:9). Let us have the attitude of the Proverb writer when he said, "Buy the truth and sell it not..." (Proverbs 23:23). Let us always remember that "lying lips are an abomination to the Lord" (Proverbs 12:22).

The Faithfulness of God

God manifests His truthfulness in His faithfulness. Faithfulness never fluctuates with God, as it does with man; He is eternally dependable. In every direction, in our present society, we see unfaithfulness:

(1) Between husbands and wives.
(2) In business dealings.
(3) In the Lord's service.
(4) In social issues.
(5) In government officials; etc.

One man recently said, "You can't trust anybody today." It is encouraging to know that in the midst of an "unfaithful generation," we can lift our eyes to the faithful God of heaven Who never changes.

Many passages attest to the faithfulness of God. Note some of the following:

Know therefore that Jehovah thy God, he is God, the faithful God, who keepeth covenant and lovingkindness... (Deuteronomy 7:9).

Thy lovingkindness, O Jehovah, is in the heavens; Thy faithfulness reacheth unto the skies (Psalm 36:5).

O Jehovah God of hosts, Who is a mighty One, like unto thee, O Jehovah? And thy faithfulness is round about thee (Psalm 89:8).

If we are faithless, he abideth faithful; for he cannot deny himself (II Timothy 2:13).

The following passages illustrate some areas of God's faithfulness:

(1) In His testimonies and commandments (Psalm 119:138).

(2) In keeping His promises (Hebrews 10:23; Moses; Exodus 3:12,21; 4:12; 33:14; Joshua 1:5; 23:14; etc.).

(3) In providing help in time of temptation (I Corinthians 10:13).

(4) In preserving His people (I Corinthians 1:9; I Thessalonians 5:24; II Timothy 2:19; the remnant of Israel; etc.):

(5) In disciplining His children (Hebrews 12:3-13).

(6) In helping the sufferer (Psalm 89:32,33; I Peter 4:19).

(7) In time of trouble (Job 5:19).

As children of a faithful Father, we must be faithful, too. Notice some areas we must be faithful in:

1. Christian living (Revelation 2:10; II Peter 1:1-9).
2. Marriage relationship (Matthew 19:4-10).
3. Stewardship (I Corinthians 4:2).
4. Ministry (Ephesians 6:1; Galatians 4:7).
5. Work (III John 5).
6. Testimony and speech (Proverbs 14:5).
7. Demonstrating it (Psalm 40:10).

Faithfulness is demonstrated time after time in the eleventh chapter of Hebrews. A careful reading of this great chapter is a must as an incentive for faithfulness. The following men exemplified faithfulness:

(1) Abraham (Genesis 22:1ff; Galatians 3:9).

(2) Joseph (Genesis 39:4,22,23).

(3) Moses (Numbers 12:7; Hebrews 3:5).

(4) David (I Samuel 22:14).

(5) Hannaniah (Nehemiah 7:2).

(6) Daniel (Daniel 6:4).
(7) Paul (Acts 20:20,27).
(8) Timothy (I Corinthians 4:17).
(9) Tychicus (Ephesians 6:21).

Let us declare with Jeremiah, "It is of Jehovah's lovingkindnesses that we are not consumed, because his compassions fail not. They are new every morning; great is thy faithfulness" (Lamentations 3:22,23). May it be said of us, in some way—Great is thy faithfulness!

The Patience of God

The Bible declares that God is a God of patience: "Now the God of patience and of comfort grant you to be of the same mind one with another according to Christ Jesus" (Romans 15:5). The patience of God is illustrated in His longsuffering toward man. It is difficult to distinguish between God's mercy, goodness, and patience. Charnock defines God's patience in the following quote:

It is part of the divine goodness and mercy, yet differs from both. God being the greatest goodness, hath the greatest mildness; mildness is always the companion of true goodness, and the greater the goodness, the greater the mildness. Who is so holy as Christ, and who is so meek? God's slowness to anger is a branch or slip from his mercy: Psalm 114:8, 'The Lord is full of compassion, slow to anger.' Only Jehovah possesses perfect patience in every situation. He alone has the power to control Himself in bearing with the wicked and restraining His punishment of them. Nahum, the prophet, said, "The Lord is slow to anger and great in power" (Nahum 1:3).

How contrasting is the patience of men. Many times when a person manifests patience, he is viewed as a coward, feeble, or weak in strength. On the other hand, many find the virtue of patience an impossibility. How many homes, lives, opportunities, etc., have been lost because of impatience? Scores! It is not possible to know how many wars may have been prevented if patience had been exercised. It is not possible, likewise, to know how many marriages could have been saved if patience had existed.

In the Old Testament, the phrase "slow to anger" is used to denote God's patience and longsuffering. Nehemiah, in discussing Israel's unfaithfulness to Jehovah, said:

And refused to obey, neither were mindful of thy wonders that thou didst among them, but hardened their neck, and in their rebellion appointed a captain to return to their bondage.
But thou art a God ready to pardon, gracious and merciful, slow to anger, and abundant in lovingkindness, and forsookest them not (Nehemiah 9:17; read the rest of the chapter).

When Israel had sinned at Kadesh-Barnea, it provoked God to say unto Moses, "How long will this people despise me? and how long will they not believe in me, for the signs which I have wrought among them? I will smite them with the pestilence, and disinherit them, and will make thee a nation greater and mightier than they" (Numbers 14:11,12). In reply to this, Moses appealed to the patience of God. He said, "...let the power of the Lord be great, according as thou hast spoken, saying, Jehovah is slow to anger, and abundant in lovingkindness, forgiving iniquity..." (Numbers 14:17,18). God's patience caused Him to sustain great injuries without immediately avenging Himself. His justice is manifested in His patience toward Israel (Acts 13:18).

Paul reminds us in Romans, chapter 9, verse 22, of God's longsuffering toward sinners; he said, "What if God will to show his wrath, and to make his power known, endured with much longsuffering vessels of wrath fitted unto destruction." Peter said, "That aforetime were disobedient, when the longsuffering of God waited in the days of Noah, while the ark was a preparing..." (I Peter 3:20). It was the patience of God that endured with these sinners. God's patience, likewise, is manifested toward us. Peter said, "The Lord...is longsuffering to you-ward, not wishing that any should perish, but that all should come to repentance" (II Peter 3:9). We must never forget that God is still patient with the world today, and is patiently waiting for us to tell every creature the Good News (Mark 16:15,16).

As followers of Christ, we are admonished to be patient:
(1) In love (I Timothy 6:11).
(2) In trials (James 1:3-5; 5:7-11).
(3) In faith (Revelation 13:10; II Thessalonians 1:4).
(4) In bearing fruit (Luke 8:15).
(5) In well-doing (Romans 2:7).
(6) In hope (I Thessalonians 1:3).
(7) In running the Christian race (Hebrews 12:1).
(8) In self-control (II Peter 1:6).
(9) In suffering (I Peter 2:20).
(10) In peril (II Corinthians 6:4-10).

In order to understand what patience is, it would be well to read the book of Job and see the patience of a suffering man (James 5:11).

The Justice of God

God's justice is based upon His immutable, Divine nature. The word for **justice** comes from the same Greek **(dike, dikaios)** and Hebrew **(tsedeq, tsaddiq)** words that are many times translated "righteousness." In the New Testament, the words "just" and "righteous" are used to convey the idea of justice. Therefore, when we consider God's justice, we are also considering His righteousness. Abraham, in dealing with God's justice toward the righteous and unrighteous, said, "Shall not the judge of all the earth do right?" (Genesis 18:25). Abraham knew that God would not punish the righteous along with the unrighteous. To do so would be unjust. God, in every situation, will always do what is right. There are many examples in the Bible of God's protection and care of the righteous:
(1) Lot (Genesis 18 and 19; cf. II Peter 2:7,8).
(2) David (I Samuel 17:37; Psalm 23).
(3) Daniel (Daniel 6:22).
(4) Peter (Acts 12:11).

(5) Paul (Acts 27:21-25).

(6) Noah (Genesis 9; II Peter 2:5).

The protection of the righteous is only one example of God's justice among men.

Justice, as a general rule in our society, has to do with one's conduct in his dealings and relations with others. Justice also involves establishing and maintaining the rights of others. Of all the virtues needed by men today, justice heads the list. You do not have to look very far today to see injustices of all kinds. Daniel Webster has eloquently stated the importance of justice in human society:

"Justice is the great interest of man on earth. It is the ligament which holds civilized beings and civilized nations together. Wherever her temple stands, and so long as it is duly honored, there is a foundation for social security, general happiness, and the improvement and progress of the race." [3] Because God is just, He has always demanded that His followers be just. We must be just in:

(1) Business dealings (Leviticus 19:35,36; Deuteronomy 25:13-16; Amos 8:5; Proverbs 11:1; 16:11; Ezekiel 45:9,10).

(2) Court actions that involve the poor, rich, strangers, etc. (Deuteronomy 16:18-20; Exodus 23:1-9).

(3) Helping the oppressed, orphans, and widows (Isaiah 1:17; 11:4; Jeremiah 22:15,16; Psalm 82:2-4; Ezekiel 18:5).

(4) Speech and actions toward others (Proverbs 10:20; 20:7; Ezekiel 18:5).

(5) Every situation under every circumstance!

Injustice was one of the reasons that God punished Israel; it contributed to their being taken into captivity. (Read the Prophets.)

The idea of justice or righteousness (remembering that these are essentially the same) becomes more spiritual and ethical in the New Testament. It is a matter of character, and God's own spirit is the standard (I John 3:7; Matthew 5:48). The mere give- and-take justice is not enough. We are to be merciful, and that to all. The idea is righteousness, not rights. As Holtzman says, 'the keynote of the Sermon On The Mount is **justitia** and not **jus.**' 4. The Christian, above all men, should be a man of justice and righteousness.

Because God loves righteousness, He executes absolute justice and judgment. This is seen in His fair punishment of the wicked, and proper justification of the righteous. Jehovah is the only judge that has a perfect sense of right and wrong; He has the "whole" truth in every situation. In His justice and judgments it is not possible for Him to be a respecter of persons and show partiality; likewise, He cannot be bribed to act contrary to truth and proper justice. This is not to say, however, that God's justice is not coupled with mercy—it most certainly is. He is "a just God and a Saviour" (Isaiah 45:21). We can rest assured that God will always uphold righteousness in every situation (Deuteronomy 10:17,18; Psalm 89:14; 97:2). In the long ago, Bildad asked, "Doth God pervert judgment? or doth the Almighty pervert justice?" (Job 8:2). The answer is, No! The Psalmist said, "Justice and judgment are the habitation of thy throne: mercy and truth shall go before thy face" (Psalm 89:14). God is a merciful, but just, Judge.

In the Old Testament, Jehovah is seen as the Just God and Savior of Israel in a national and temporal sense. In the New Testament, Jesus Christ is seen as the Just God and Savior in the spiritual sense. Peter referred to the Savior as "the Holy One and the Just" (Acts 3:14). Many times in the New Testament, Christ is referred to as judge (John 5:22,27,30; Acts 17:30,31; Romans 14:10; II Corinthians 5:10). God's justice and righteousness are fully realized in His forgiveness of sins. "It is by the forgiveness of sins that God establishes righteousness, and this is the supreme task of justice. Thus it is that God is at the same time 'just, and the justifier of him that hath faith in Jesus' " (Romans 3:26). John said, "He is faithful and righteous [just—JJT] to forgive us our sins, and to cleanse us from all unrighteousness" (I John 1:9). How wonderful to know that our Judge has paid our "fine" with His own precious blood (I Peter 1:18,19; Acts 20:28; John 3:16) and thereby, upon our appropriating that blood by obedience (Romans 6:1-6), pronounces us—**not guilty!** Truly, our Judge is a just judge.

The Wrath of God:

God's holiness will not permit Him to look upon sin. "Art not thou from everlasting, O Jehovah, my God, my Holy One?...Thou art of purer eyes than to behold evil" (Habakkuk 1:12,13). Therefore, because God hates sin (Nahum 1:2; Psalm 5:5), and is just in dealing with man, He must by His very nature of holiness punish the evil doer. Of all the attributes of God, none is rejected as easily as His wrath. Many so-called Christians reject the wrath of God; some are perplexed about it; still others wish it did not exist. The atheist usually believes that evil, which he considers God's wrath to be, proves that there is no God—especially a good and holy one. His question is: How can God's holiness and goodness be harmonized with His wrath and other evils in the world? It is shallow thinking or close mindedness to conclude that God's goodness and holiness must cancel out His justice. Goodness and holiness demand justice! Jehovah would not be good or holy if he failed to render justice toward the righteous and unrighteous. Who is ready to call a judge **good** that never renders a verdict to punish the evildoer? Only the criminal!

The Bible makes it clear that God is a God of wrath. Notice the following passages:

See now that I, even I, am he, And there is no god with me:
I kill, and I make alive; I wound, and I heal; And there is none that can deliver out of my hand...If I whet my glittering sword,
And my hand take hold on judgment; I will render vengeance to mine adversaries, And will recompense them that hate me (Deuteronomy 32:39,41).

For the wrath of God is revealed from heaven against all ungodliness and unrighteousness of men... (Romans 1:28).

Wherefore I sware in my wrath, That they should not enter into my rest (Psalm 95:11; cf. Hebrews 3:12).

But after that our fathers had provoked the God of heaven unto wrath, he gave them into the hand of Nebuchadnezzar king of Babylon... (Ezra 5:12).

If is a fearful thing to fall into the hands of the living God (Hebrews 10:31).

For God is a consuming Fire (Hebrews 12:29).

...he treadeth the winepress of the fierceness of the wrath of God, the Almighty (Revelation 19:15).

God's wrath is free from injustice and unethical, hasty qualities. Jehovah is not an impulsive Judge, as the heathen gods were viewed to be. The wrath of man usually stems from his enraged sinful attitude or nature; this wrath is condemned in the Bible (Genesis 4:5,6; 49:7; Proverbs 19:19; Job 5:2; Luke 4:28; II Corinthians 12:10; Galatians 5:20; Ephesians 4:31; Colossians 3:8). Man must not "give place unto wrath" (Ephesians 4:26). The father, likewise, must not provoke his children to wrath (Ephesians 6:1-4). We must be careful not to think of God as altogether as we are, especially in the area of wrath (Psalm 50:21).

The Divine wrath is to be regarded as the natural expression of the Divine nature, which is absolute holiness, manifesting itself against the willful, highhanded, deliberate, inexcusable sin and iniquity.

The sin of Adam and Eve illustrates God's justice. After creating them, God gave them a positive divine law (Genesis 2:16,17), which also included the penalty for violating the law: "...thou shalt not eat of it: for in the day that thou eatest thereof **thou shalt surely die."** Therefore, from the very beginning, the justice and goodness of God is seen. The next test for God after giving this law is a test of His truthfulness—will He keep His word? A reading of Genesis 3:9-24 will reveal that He did. A careful reading of the Bible will also reveal that God always revealed what was required, as well as the punishment for not doing what was required (e.g., Leviticus 26; Deuteronomy 29, 30). This is true justice!

Man's failure to understand the severity (Romans 11:22) of God may stem from his failure to see the enormity and sinfulness of sin. Men have a tendency to regard sin lightly, to cover up its ugliness, and make excuses for it. The more we study God's holiness, the more we shall be able to understand the heinousness of sin and why one sin is sufficient to separate us from God (Isaiah 59:1,2). Sin is rebellion against God's holiness, sovereignty, and authority. Therefore, it demands punishment.

Here are but a few examples of God's punishment of the wrongdoer:

(1)　　Adam and Eve (Genesis 2 and 3).
(2)　　Cain (Genesis 4).
(3)　　The ancient world (Genesis 7-9; II Peter 2:6).
(4)　　Angels (II Peter 2:4).
(5)　　Sodom and Gomorrah (II Peter 2:6).
(6)　　Israel (Hebrews 3:7-9; Numbers 14:29ff).
(7)　　Nineveh (Book of Nahum, etc.).
(8)　　Ananias and Sapphira (Acts 5:1-6).
(9)　　Nadab and Abihu (Leviticus 10:1,2).
(10)　　Korah (Numbers 16:1-3, 31-35; Jude 11).

In these examples, and all others that may be appealed to, punishment came because of sin and rebellion. Time after time, the Judge of all the earth is seen doing that which is right (Genesis 18:25).

Since God is holy and just, how shall the ungodly stand in the judgment? (Psalm 1:5). "If the Lord shouldest mark [impute—JJT] iniquities, O Lord, who shall stand?" (Psalm 130:3). This is the dilemma of all men (Romans 3:23; 6:23; John 8:24; etc.). The eternal question is: How shall we escape the wrath of God? We **all** deserve it because of our sins. The good news is: God can forgive sins because of the atonement made by Jesus Christ, His only begotten Son (John 1:29; Matthew 26:28; I John 2:2; Revelation 1:5; Hebrews 9, 10). Because of God's grace, we are not punished as soon as we sin; and because of His mercy and our acceptance of Christ as our sacrifice for sin, we will not be punished in eternity. Let us turn to Christ and flee from the wrath that is to come (Matthew 3:7; II Thessalonians 1:7-9). It is a fearful thing to fall into the hands of the living God (Hebrews 10:31).

The Grace and Mercy of God:

God's grace (Greek **chart***) is His unmerited favor toward sinners; His mercy (Greek **eleos**) is divine compassion manifested toward the miserable and distressed. "Grace has respect to sinful man as guilty, while mercy has respect to him as miserable." [7] In the Old Testament, the mercy of God was made known unto Israel by the Hebrew words **hesedh,** which is usually translated **kindness** or **lovingkindness,** and **hanan,** which is usually translated **to be gracious, to be inclined to,** and **mercy.** Note the following passages:

Jehovah, a God merciful and gracious, slow to anger, and abundant in lovingkindness... (Exodus 34:6).

For Jehovah thy God is a merciful God; he will not fail thee, neither destroy thee, nor forget the covenant of thy fathers which he sware unto them (Deuteronomy 4:31).

...I will be gracious to whom I will be gracious, and will show mercy on whom I will show mercy (Exodus 33:19).

...Thou hast shown unto thy servant...great lovingkindness... (I Kings 3:6).

Oh give thanks unto Jehovah; for he is good; for his lovingkindness endureth forever (Psalm 136:1).

As we study God's mercy, let us not confuse it with emotional permissiveness, or as something we deserve. God is merciful because of

His grace.

Because God is a just God, He must punish sinners. Justice demands it. Since this is true, how is it possible for God to remain just and still pardon the condemned sinner? The apostle Paul states how this is possible:

Being justified freely by his grace through the redemption that is in Christ Jesus: whom God set forth to be a propitiation, through faith, in his blood, to show his righteousness at this present season: that he might himself be just, and the justifier of him that hath faith in Jesus (Romans 3:24-26).

In these great verses, Paul declares that God is a just Judge because He paid the price of our freedom by sending His own Son to shed His blood for our redemption. Therefore, God's wrath has been satisfied by His grace and mercy which sent His Son into the world to die on a cross. It is upon the basis of Christ's sacrifice upon the cross that all men, of all ages, may be justified (Hebrews 9:15-22). God's unmerited favor, as far as the Bible reveals, has only been extended to fallen man. It is not extended to fallen angels, demons, or the devil (II Peter 2:4; Matthew 25:41). It is only with man, who is created in His image, that Jehovah has been forbearing and longsuffering (Exodus 34:6; Romans 2:4,5; 9:22,23; I Peter 3:20; II Peter 3:9,15).

The Bible makes it very clear that salvation stems from God's grace and mercy:

For by grace have ye been saved through faith; and not of yourselves, it is the gift of God; not of works, that no man should glory (Ephesians 2:8,9).

For God hath shut up all unto disobedience, that he might have mercy upon all (Romans 11:32).

Not by works done in righteousness, which we did ourselves, but according to his mercy he saved us, through the washing of regeneration and renewing of the Holy Spirit (Titus 3:5,6).

For I will be merciful to their iniquities, And their sins will I remember no more (Hebrews 8:12).

It should be remembered, however, that because salvation is made possible by God's grace, it does not rule out man's acceptance of that grace by faithful obedience. The Hebrew writer said, "And having been made perfect, he [Jesus—JJT] became unto all them that **obey** him the author of eternal salvation" (Hebrews 5:9). Therefore, through faith, repentance, confession, and baptism, a man puts on Christ (John 8:24; Luke 13:3; Matthew 10:32,33; Mark 16:16; Galatians 3:27) and becomes a new creature (John 3:3-5; Titus 3:5,6). In obedience, the fallen man has accepted God's grace.

It is clearly revealed in the Scriptures that the Triune Godhead shares in the administration of grace and mercy toward sinners in bringing about their salvation. The following passages show the work of the Father, Son, and Holy Spirit in bringing about the redemption of fallen man:

(1) **Father:** For **God** so loved the world, that he **gave** his only begotten Son... (John 3:16, etc.).

(2) **Son: Jesus...** by the grace of God he should taste of **death** for every man (Hebrews 5:9; cf. John 1:29; Matthew 26:28; Revelation 1:5; 5:5-10; I John 2:2).

(3) **Holy Spirit:** He **saved** us through the washing of **regeneration** and renewing of the Holy Spirit (Titus 3:5; cf. John 3:3-5). So **belief** cometh of **hearing,** and hearing by the **word** of Christ (Romans 10:17). And take the helmet of salvation, and the sword of the **Spirit,** which is the **word** of God (Ephesians 6:17).

This point will be studied in more detail in lessons 8-13 of our study.

Since we have been extended mercy, we in turn must extend mercy toward others. Jesus said, "Blessed are the merciful: for they shall obtain mercy" (Matthew 5:7). James said, "For judgment is without mercy to him that hath showed no mercy: mercy glorieth against judgment" (James 2:13). Therefore, since mercy has been extended to us, let us be "kind one to another, tenderhearted, forgiving each other, even as God also in Christ forgave you" (Ephesians 4:32). "For if ye forgive men their trespasses, your heavenly Father will also forgive you" (Matthew 5:14). Micah, the prophet, makes it clear that God has always desired mercy (Micah 6:6-8). Let us strive to be more merciful toward one another. May we always remember that God's "lovingkindness is great unto the heavens" (Psalm 57:10).

Conclusion

"Praise the Lord, ye heavens, adore Him!
Praise Him angels, in the height;
Sun and moon rejoice before Him;
Praise Him, all ye stars of light...
Praise the God of our salvation;
Hosts on high, His power proclaim; Heaven
and earth, and all creation,
Laud and magnify His name."
(J. Kempthorne and L. Mason Psalm 148:1,2)

QUESTIONS FOR DISCUSSION

1. Discuss the modern day attitude toward lying. Do you agree with the newspaper article about lying 17 times each day?
2. Why is lying so easy? Who originated lying?
3. Why must God be truthful?
4. Discuss faithfulness in the home and church.
5. Why must God be faithful?
6. What is your definition of patience? Discuss.
7. In your opinion, what one thing best illustrates God's patience?
8. How can one develop patience? Discuss.
9. Define "justice."
10. What is God's justice based upon?
11. Discuss justice in the courts of today.

12. Upon what basis are Christians pronounced "Not Guilty"?
13. Discuss some improper concepts of God's wrath.
14. Would God be just if He didn't punish the evildoer? Discuss.
15. Why is evil in the world?
16. Discuss grace and mercy.
17. Discuss grace and obedience.
18. How is grace misunderstood by many today?

FOOTNOTES

[1] H. D. M. Spence and Joseph S. Exell, Editor, *The Pulpit Commentary* (Grand Rapids, MI: Wm. B. Eerdman Pub. Co., 1963 reprint), Vol. 13, "Hosea," p. 358.

[2] Stephen Charnock, *The Existence and Attributes of God* (Grand Rapids, MI: Sovereign Grace Publishers, 1971), p. 764.

[3] Tryon Edwards, Compiler, *The New Dictionary of Thoughts* (Standard Book Co.), p. 327.

[4] Harris Franklin Rail, "Justice" in *International Standard Bible Encyclopedia,* ed. James Orr (Grand Rapids: Wm. B. Eerdman Publishing Company, 1956), 3:1782.

[5] Ibid, p. 1782.

[6] Ibid, Vol. 5, p. 3113.

Henry C. Thiessen, *Lectures in Systematic Theology* (Grand Rapids, MI: Wm. B. Eerdman Pub. Co., 1949), p. 132.

Chapter Eight
THE PRE-EXISTENCE OF CHRIST

Introduction:

In Matthew 22:42, Jesus asked the Pharisees, "What think ye of the Christ? whose son is he?" On another occasion he asked, "Who do men say that the Son of man is?" (Matthew 16:13). The answer to these questions is inevitable when we hear Peter declare, "Thou art the Christ, the son of the living God!" (Matthew 16:16).

It is understood in this declaration that the Deity of Christ is confessed. Concerning the Divinity of Jesus, Robert Milligan, late President of the College of the Bible in Kentucky University, wrote,

"Was he mere man having no existence prior to his conception by the virgin Mary...Or did he exist in any other state of conscious personality previous to that time? If so, to what rank or order of beings did he belong? Was he a creature of some angelic or super-angelic order...Or was he an uncreated Aeon, or emanation from the Deity...Or was he God himself, one with the Father in essence, and endowed with all the attributes of Divinity, but nevertheless having his own separate and distinct personality...?".1

If it be true that Jesus is the Divine Son of God, and it is, then we must attend to a diligent study of that divine personality prior to His earthly existence. We shall limit ourselves to the following areas for study:

(1) Jesus' testimony concerning His pre-existence;
(2) John's testimony concerning the pre-existence of Christ;
(3) Paul's testimony concerning the pre-existence of Christ;
(4) Peter's testimony concerning the pre-existence of Christ;
(5) The Holy Spirit's testimony concerning the pre-existence of Christ.

Jesus' Testimony for His Pre-existence:

Recorded in the Gospels is Jesus' own affirmation: "All things have been delivered unto Me of My Father; and no one knoweth the Son save the Father; neither doth any know the Father, save the Son, and he to whomsoever the Son willeth to reveal him (Matthew 11:25-27; Luke 10:21-22).

In this Jesus declares that there is a special relationship between him and the Father. Jesus recognized this and declared, "I and the Father are one" (John 10:30). He affirmed His own Deity when he claimed:

(1) Heaven was His native country (John 3:13; 6:33,50,51).

(2) He knew from whence He came and to where He was going (John 8:14).

(3) That the One who sent Him the Jews knew not (John 7:28-29).

(4) The Father sent Him into the world (John 8:36).

(5) That He came from the Father and would return to the Father (John 16:28).

(6) The Son receives honor as does the Father (John 5:23).

His affirmation concerning His Deity is further heightened by His claim, "Before Abraham was, I am" (John 8:58). This language can only be seen as a direct affirmation from Christ regarding His pre-existence. In His prayer to the Father, He stated, "And now, O Father, glorify Thou Me with Thine own self with the glory I had with Thee before the world was" (John 17:4-5). And further, "Thou lovedst Me before the foundation of the world" (John 17:24).

Therefore, while in the form of human flesh, Jesus gives us a glimpse of divine glory, as He affirms that He is the Divine Son of God.

John's Testimony Concerning The Pre-existence of Christ:

John presents Jesus as the Divine, Eternal Son of God. This is the substance of John **1:1-18.** John refers to Jesus as the **logos** or the Word (cf. John 1:1 with John 1:14). In presenting the **logos,** John says the **logos** held a special relationship with God. This relationship is described as:

(1) **Eternal—"In the beginning."** This carries us back to a time prior to human history or of temporal things. The fact of pre-existence is not directly stated but is definitely implied, in that the **logos** was already in existence when "the beginning" first started.

(2) **Personal—"and the Word [Logos] was with God."** This statement definitely implies an intimate relationship. The term "with" is used to imply an association in the sense of free mingling with the others of a community on terms of equality. Alexander observes, "The preposition **with** expresses beyond the fact of coexistence that of perpetual intercommunion." This simply means that John is here expressing that the **logos** has always had a special communion (fellowship) with the Father.

(3) **Divine—"and the word was God."** The word translated God is the word **Theos**. It is used in a particular sense in this passage of scripture. Here the word is used without the article. John did not say that the **logos** was **"the God"** but rather the **logos was God.** When the article is omitted in the original language in connection with the word **Theos,** "the emphasis of the word is on the quality, God as a kind of being." '

W. E. Best states,

The substance of John 1:1-18 is that He who is the logos was with God and was God. Three great facts are presented in John 1:1; they are (1) **When** the word was—**'in the beginning'**; (2) **Where** the Word was—**'with God'**; (3) **Who** the Word was— **'God!'** " '

He continues:

"Jesus Christ is the Eternal Logos. He was not from the beginning; He already was in the beginning. He was not only with God; He was God. No exegetical jugglery can hide the force of the truth contained in John 1:1. As a word may be distinguished from the thought it expresses (for the two are not identical), so can the second person of the Godhead be distinguished from the first. There cannot be a word apart from the thought behind it; neither an apprehension of the existence of 'God' and the 'Word' without another. They are distinguishable but inseparable. 4

John further adds to his testimony when he writes, "That which was from the beginning, that which we have heard, that which we have seen with our eyes, that which we beheld, and our hands handled, concerning the Word of life" (I John 1:1-3).

Truly, as recorded by John, we shall say with Thomas, "My Lord and my God!" (John 20:28). For John adds his endorsement to the fact that Jesus existed as God (Deity) prior to the beginning.

Paul's Testimony for the Pre-existence of Christ

In Colossians 2:9, Paul gives concise and clear support to the Deity of Jesus when he states, "for in him [Christ] dwelleth all the fulness of the Godhead bodily." To give proper emphasis to this passage we need to look at three words.

(1) The word for fulness is the word **pleroma.** This word is defined in the following ways: (1) "Denotes fulness, that of which a thing is full"; [5] (2) "That which is (has been) filled"; [6] and (3) "That which is full of something."[7] By definition, the meaning of the word is that something is full of whatever is talked about. To express it in the negative, we might say it means to be without anything lacking. In other words, nothing is lacking to make it full or sufficient.

"Paul says that Jesus Christ is not only the chief manifestation of the divine nature. He exhaults the Godhead. In Him resides the totality of the divine powers and attributes." [8]

(2) The word for Godhead is the word **Theothetos.** This word is defined as "divinity, deity, godhead." [9]

This word is found three times in the New Testament—Acts 17:29, Romans 1:20, and Colossians 2:9. Concerning this word, Trench observes, "Paul is declaring that in the Son there dwells all the fullness of absolute Godhead; they were no mere rays of divine glory which gilded Him, lighting up His Person for a season and with splendor not His own; but He was, and is, absolute and perfect God; and the apostle uses **Theotes** to express this essential and personal Godhead of the Son."

(3) We take notice of the word **bodily**. The word is the word **somatikos**. "It dwells in him **bodily:** i.e., in bodily form or manner" "...pointing to Christ's human body, not to the church or to the created world. The fullness of the Godhead dwelt in Him as the Eternal Word (1:19) and because of this when the Word became flesh (John 1:14), the fullness dwelt in him 'bodily,' in bodily fashion." [12]

On another occasion Paul states indirectly the pre-existence of Christ when he attributes to Jesus the quality of being Deity. In Philippians 2:6, it is stated, "Who, existing in the **form** of God, counted not the being on an equality with God a thing to be grasped." The word "form" is the word **morphe** and means, "...a great deal more than the external appearance; it stands for the essence of God's nature, so that we may say that Jesus Christ possessed the essence of the Divine quality and nature from all eternity."[14]

To further show that Jesus had pre-existence, the writer of the book of Hebrews states that it was through the Son that God made the worlds (Hebrews 1:1-4), and Paul states in Colossians 1:16-17 that through Him all things were created.

With this, we must conclude with Paul that Jesus must have existed prior to His bodily form. He was not a created being but is in fact Deity that was manifested in the flesh.

Peter's Testimony for the Pre-existence of Christ:

The testimony of Peter regarding the pre-existence of the Christ comes from his first epistle, chapter one, verses eighteen and nineteen. There he states that we were redeemed

...with the precious blood, as of a lamb without blemish and without spot, even the blood of Christ: who was foreknown indeed before the foundation of the world. In order for Peter to state that Christ was the lamb of God slain for the sins before the foundation of the world, it must be assumed that Jesus had existence prior to the foundation of the world.

Thus Peter agrees with others that Jesus had an existence prior to his manifestation in the flesh.

The Holy Spirit's Testimony for the Pre-existence of Christ:

The testimony of the Holy Spirit of God regarding the pre-existence of Jesus is perhaps one of the strongest that one can study in this specific area of our quest. The Spirit of God inspired the writers of Scripture, both of the Old and New Testaments (cf. II Peter 1:20-21; II Timothy 3:16-17). By inspiration, God is revealed by a name which declares his eternal nature and being: Yahweh or Jehovah. In Exodus 6:2-3, scripture states, "I am Yahweh [Jehovah], I appeared to Abraham, Isaac, and Jacob as God Almighty, but I never made myself known to them as Yahweh [Jehovah]."

The word "Jehovah" is derived from putting the vowels of the Hebrew word **Adonah,** the word for Lord, on the four-letter word of the Hebrew **yhwh,** which is probably sounded as "Yahweh." In the Greek version of the Old Testament, it is translated by the word "Lord." The Greek form for this word is **Kurios.** This is the form read by Jesus and the Apostles, and the Jews of the first century in their Greek Bible.

There are many passages in the Old Testament where this name is used (i.e., the name Yahweh-Jehovah—Lord) which in the New Testament are clearly shown to apply to our Lord Jesus Christ. In this way the writers of the New Testament show that Jesus was considered God, because He was entitled to wear the divine name of God. Perhaps the best way to prove what is being said is to go to the scripture itself.

(1) In Isaiah 40:3, Isaiah writes, "The voice of one that crieth, Prepare ye in the wilderness the way of Jehovah; make level in the desert a highway for our God." This prophecy states that Jehovah is expected to visit the earth and that, prior to his visit, there will be a forerunner. Matthew states that the coming of John the Baptist as the forerunner of Jesus is a fulfillment of this prophecy of Isaiah. Therefore, Jesus is the Jehovah God of whom Isaiah spoke.

(2) The Psalmist declares, "O taste and see that Jehovah is gracious" (Psalm 34:8). Peter, by inspiration of the Holy Spirit, applies this to the Lord Jesus Christ in 1 Peter 2:3.

(3) Consider the words of the Apostle John as he writes in Revelation 1:17 and 22:13, when he ascribes attributes to Jesus that Isaiah the prophet asserted to Jehovah in Isaiah 44:6.

These are just a few of the examples that could be given which show that the New Testament writers spoke of Jesus as fulfilling many Old Testament passages referring to Jehovah. A listing of these, with the New Testament passages where they are fulfilled, would be in order. They are:

(1) Psalm 102:24-27, fulfilled in Hebrews 1:10-12;
(2) Isaiah 40:3, fulfilled in Matthew 3:3 and Luke 1:68,69,76;
(3) Jeremiah 11:20 and 17:10, fulfilled in Revelation 2:23;
(4) Isaiah 60:19, fulfilled in Luke 2:32;
(5) Isaiah 6:1,3,10, fulfilled in John 12:37-41;
(6) Isaiah 8:13-14, fulfilled in I Peter 2:7-8;
(7) Numbers 21:6-7, compared with I Corinthians 10:9;
(8) Psalm 23:1, compared with John 10:11; and
(9) Ezekiel 34:11-12,18, compared with Luke 19:10.

With these thoughts before us, we conclude that many passages in the Old Testament that refer to Jehovah are found to be fulfilled in the person and work of Jesus in the New Testament. Thus, the Holy Spirit (as He inspired men to write) gives His testimony to the fact that Jesus is Deity by asserting His pre-existence in that Jesus is the Jehovah of the Old Testament.

Activities of the Pre-existence Christ:

Since we have seen that Christ did exist prior to his earthly manifestation, we now conclude by noticing the activities of the pre-existent Christ:

(1) Christ was, in his pre-existent state, creator of the universe—John 1:3; Colossians 1:16-18; Hebrews 1:2,10; 2:10.

(2) He was controller of the universe—Hebrews 1:3; Colossians 1:17. This is the work of Deity. Therefore, it is seen that Jesus had a state of pre-existence rightfully His.

QUESTIONS FO DISCUSSION

Discuss what is meant by "pre-existence."

1. What do we mean when we say that Jesus is Deity?
2. Did Jesus recognize that He was Deity? How do you know?
3. Explain what is meant in John 8:58.
4. In what three ways did John say Jesus **(logos)** had a special relationship with God?
5. What one particular passage tells us Paul's greatest testimony concerning the pre-existence of Christ? Discuss this passage.
6. Does showing Jesus to be Deity **prove** His pre-existence? How? Explain.
7. Discuss Peter's testimony for the pre-existence of Christ.
8. How does the Holy Spirit show the pre-existence of Christ?
9. Discuss the two activities listed of the pre-existent Christ.

FOOTNOTES

¹Robert Milligan, *The Scheme of Redemption* (St. Louis, MO: The Bethany Press, 17th Printing, 1966), pp. 216-217.

²Merrill C. Tenney, *John—The Gospel of Belief* (Grand Rapids, MI: Wm. B. Eerdman Pub. Co., 1968), p. 65.

W. E. Best, *The Impeccable Christ* (Grand Rapids, MI: Sovereign

Grace Publishers, 1971), p. 14.

ʲIbid., p. 16.

W. E. Vine, *An Expository Dictionary of New Testament Words* (Westwood: Fleming H. Revell, 1966), Vol. 11, p. 137.

⁷Joseph Henry Thayer, *Greek-English Lexicon* (Grand Rapids, MI: Zondervan Pub. Co., 1966), p. 518.

W. F. Ardnt and F. W. Gingrich, *A Greek-English Lexicon of the New Testament* (Chicago, IL: Chicago University Press, 1957), p. 678.

"Kenneth S. Wuest, *Word Studies From the Greek New Testament* (Grand Rapids, MI: Wm. B. Eerdman Pub. Co., 1969), pp. 167-168.

^Harpers, *Analytical Greek Lexicon* (New York: Harper & Row, no date), p. 193.

¹⁰R. C. Trench, as quoted by Wuest, p. 203.

"Beet, as quoted by James D. Bales, *Paul's Approach to Colossians* (unpublished paper), p. 67.

'"Schaff, as quoted by Bales, p. 62.

"F. B. Meyer, *The Epistle to the Philippians* (Grand Rapids, MI: Baker Book House, 1952), p. 82.

ᴹWilliam Hendrickson, *New Testament Commentary Philippians* (Grand Rapids, MI: Baker Book House, 1962), p. 105.

Chapter Nine
THE INCARNATION OF CHRIST
Introduction

Sir Isaac Newton, in an attempt to describe his search for knowledge, said that he felt like a little boy walking by the seashore occasionally picking up some pebbles, while the vast, deep, unexplored and unknown rolled at his feet.

Such is the feeling of this writer as we engage in the study before us concerning the Incarnation of Christ. Since many great men of days gone by have had feelings similar to those of Newton, it would be the height of folly and presumption for this writer to feel that he could discuss exhaustively a subject of great magnitude in such a limited space.

In Matthew 13:54-55, we have the following words recorded concerning Jesus: "And coming into his own country he taught them in their synagogue, insomuch that they were astonished, and said, Whence hath this man this wisdom, and these mighty works? Is not this the carpenter's son? Is not his mother Mary? And his brethren, James, and Joseph, and Simon and Judas?"

With these words we enter into our study of the Incarnation of Christ. The words—**Is not this the carpenter's son?**—signify that those of Jesus' own country recognized that there was something different about Him. What was it? Why did the life that Jesus lived stand out so much as is evidenced by the preceding passage of Scripture? Indeed, we too ask the question—Whence hath this man wisdom and these mighty works? What made Jesus different from others, even one so great as John the Baptizer? The answer to such an investigation is a study of the Incarnation.

Definition

Our word **Incarnation** comes from the Latin and means literally "embodiment or the assumption of humanity." ' The Incarnation, then, is a study of God being manifested in human flesh. This was the testimony of John in John 1:14, "And the Word became flesh, and dwelt among us." Concerning the Incarnation, Boettner observes, "In the Incarnation God was born a babe in Bethlehem. For a period of thirty-three years that union continued in a form which manifested the human much more clearly than the Divine, although on numerous occasions the Divine made itself manifest through supernatural works. Particularly on the mount of transfiguration the veil was partially removed and the Divine showed out in its true glory. But with the resurrection and ascension human nature, by virtue of its union with Deity, was glorified far beyond anything of which it was capable in this world." *

However, lest we not really be aware of it, let it be stated here (which will be developed in this chapter) that a study of the Incarnation is a study of the Doctrine of Salvation.

Our study of the Incarnation will be presented in the follow ing manner:

(1) The importance of the Incarnation;
(2) The testimony of the Scriptures concerning the Incarnation;
(3) The testimony of the Virgin Birth concerning the Incarnation;
(4) What the Incarnation involved; and
(5) The purpose of the Incarnation.

The Importance of the Incarnation of Christ:

In I Timothy 3:16, Paul exclaimed:

"And without controversy great is the mystery of godliness; He [God—KJV] who was manifested in the flesh, justified in the spirit, seen of angels, preached among the nations, believed on in the world, received up in glory."

The Incarnation of Christ is a foundation upon which all of Christianity rests. So important is a belief in the Incarnation that John says, "...every spirit that confesseth that Jesus Christ is come in the flesh is of God: and every spirit that confesseth not Jesus is not of God: and this is the spirit of the antichrist" (I John 4:2-3).

John, more than any other, in his Gospel and writings gives testimony to the importance of the Incarnation. Someone asks, "Why is a study of the Incarnation of Jesus so important?" The answer is—It is important because there are some who deny that Jesus Christ is God manifested in the flesh.

In John 1:14, the scripture states, "And the Word became flesh and dwelt among us." This Word is Christ. Jesus Christ was Divine and manifested Deity in the flesh (cf. John 1:1-3,14; Philippians 2:5-11).

In I John 4:2-3, John stresses the importance of the Incarnation when he states that to deny Jesus being manifested in the flesh is to be: (1) "not of God;" and (2) "of the antichrist." To deny that Jesus is God manifested in the flesh is a gross error, for it is to deny the very basis of Christianity. (This we shall see later in this study under the heading "The Purpose of the Incarnation.")

Dr. John T. Ritchie Smith states,

God may assume the form of man because man was made in the likeness of God. The Eternal Word may become the Son of Man because man is by **nature** the son of God. He could not take upon Him a nature wholly foreign to His own, nor become that which is altogether unlike Himself. [1] When man sinned in Paradise Garden, he cut himself off from God and made himself incapable of renewing the relationship he once enjoyed. Thus Christ, in His infinite mercy, assumed this task for him. Jesus clothed himself in human flesh so that He might be man's sacrifice and thereby satisfy the Divine demand for justice. Only a human could suffer and die, and only a Divine person could give that suffering infinite value. The Hebrew writer put it this way,

Since then the children are sharers in flesh and blood, **He also Himself in like manner partook of the same** (emphasis mine, EPM), that through death He...might deliver all them who through fear of death were all their lifetime subject to bondage... Wherefore it behooved Him in all things **to be made like unto his brethren, that he might become a merciful and faithful high priest in things pertaining to God** (emphasis mine, EPM), to make propitiation for the sins of the people" (Hebrews 2:14-17).

Indeed, Paul was right—**great is the mystery of Godliness!** (I Timothy 3:16). The Bible does not question the Incarnation but merely states it as a fact. Yet it is mysterious to understand. However, one need not take the position that, because the Incarnation is a mystery to understand, it cannot be true. The Bible explains the Incarnation of Christ in the simplest of words, and yet never seeks to give the subject detailed explanation.

"In the beginning was the Word and the Word was with God and the Word was God." "And the Word became flesh." That means that God became a man! What simple words, and yet who can explain them? Who understands them? Nobody!

Who knows everything there is to know about God? You don't, nobody ever has, and nobody ever will. Now I may know something about God that you don't know, or you might know something about God that I don't, or somebody might know something about God that neither you nor I know, but **nobody** knows everything that there is about God! There are some things about God that neither you nor I nor anybody will ever know. Therefore, God is a mystery. And yet, there are some things about God that we all can know, for they have been revealed to us in Sacred Scripture.

The Testimony of the Scriptures to the Incarnation:

The Scriptures give their testimony to the Incarnation of Christ. It begins with Old Testament prophecy predicting His birth (Genesis 3:15; Isaiah 7:14; 9:6; et al.) and continues with the writers of the New Testament giving record of what Jesus said of His own existence and Incarnation. Notice in the Scripture what is said by Jesus Himself concerning His nature:

(1) **Scripture records that Jesus talks about the fact that the Messiah possessed a dual nature** (cf. Matthew **22:41-43;** Mark **12:35-37).** True, Jesus was the son of David, but He was also the Son of God. Jesus was trying to get those to whom He was talking to see that the Messiah not only possessed a human nature but also a Divine nature.

(2) **Scripture gives testimony when it records that Jesus claimed for Himself to be God manifested in the flesh.** Jesus stated that He came from heaven and therefore was Divine in His nature (cf. John 6:33; 6:38; 8:23; 8:42; et al.).

(3) Scripture records testimony concerning the Incarnation when it records that Jesus said that God sent Him to do the work that He was doing. (Read John 8:29; 8:42; 8:18.)

(4) **Scripture gives testimony when it records that Jesus is referred to as both the Son of Man and the Son of God.** Seventy-seven times in the New Testament, Jesus is referred to as the "Son of Man." And yet, the Bible just as clearly calls him the Son of God.

Paul states that Jesus was a son born according to the flesh and yet declared to be the Son of God with power by the resurrection from the dead (cf. Romans 1:3-4).

Jesus recognized his dual nature and stated, "We must work the works of Him that sent me while it is yet day; for the night cometh when no man can work" (John 9:4).

Paul states, "There is one mediator between God and man, **Himself man,** Christ Jesus" (I Timothy 2:5). And yet Thomas declares to Him, "My Lord and My God!" (John 20:26-28).

Therefore, we must conclude from Scripture that the Bible teaches Jesus was both human and Divine.

The Testimony of the Virgin Birth Concerning the Incarnation:

There is a very definite relationship between the Incarnation and the Virgin Birth. Luke records, "And the Angel answered and said unto her, the Holy Spirit shall come upon thee, and the power of the

Most High shall overshadow thee: wherefore also the holy thing which is begotten shall be called the Son of God (Luke 1:35).

Matthew records that the birth of Jesus by a virgin would bring the Christ into the world who would be "Immanuel, God with us!" (Matthew 1:18-23).

There was a necessity of a Divine and human parent if Jesus were to possess a dual nature. Without the Virgin Birth, the Incarnation would not have been possible.

What the Incarnation Involved:

Involved in the Incarnation was the union of two natures—one human and the other divine. This is, perhaps, one of the deepest thoughts in our study of the Incarnation. Concerning the human nature, the following is involved:

(1) **The Incarnation involved a human birth.** The Bible speaks of Jesus being born of woman (Galatians 4:4). The record of this is found in Matthew 1:18—2:12 and Luke 1:30-38 and 2:1-20.

(2) **The Incarnation involved human development.** If Jesus is God manifested **in the flesh,** He must of necessity develop as a human being. The Scripture states that He "grew and waxed strong, filled with wisdom: and the grace of God was upon Him" (Luke 2:40), and that He "advanced in wisdom and stature, and in favor with God and men" (Luke 2:52). Jesus was a man with the human nature of a man. He developed as a man. Becoming a man was a necessity in order for him to be touched with the feeling of our infirmities. (Read Hebrews 4:15.)

(3) **The Incarnation involved Jesus having human characteristics.** By this we mean that He must have the appearance of a man. He must look, act, feel, and be seen as a man. To see this, one should study carefully the following passages of Scripture: Philippians 2:5-11; Matthew 14:24-27; Luke 24:36-43; John 4:9, 20:15, and 20:19-20.

(4) **The incarnation involved Jesus having human limitation.** As a

man, he was subject to the limitations of men. This He was, for according to Scripture:

(a) He hungered (Matthew 21:18).
(b) He thirsted (John 4:7; 19:28).
(c) He became weary and needed sleep (John 4:6; Matthew 8:24).
(d) He experienced pain and death (1 Peter 3:18 and 4:1; I Corinthians 15:3).
(e) He learned obedience (Hebrews 5:8).
(f) He was subject to testing and trials (Matthew 4:1; Hebrews 4:15).
(g) He prayed (Mark 1:35; Luke 11:1).
(h) He had human recognition. He was referred to as: (a) Jesus of Nazareth (Luke 18:27; 24:19; John 18:5; Acts 22:8); (i)the Son of Joseph (Matthew 13:55; Luke 3:23); and (j) the Son of Man (Matthew 26:63-64; John 1:49-51).

With this vast amount of evidence, would one be so bold as to deny that Jesus existed as a man? If Jesus did not really become incarnate, the Bible surely goes to a lot of trouble to show that He did. Let the doubter explain that!

The other union involved in the Incarnation was the Divine union. Suffice it to say here that Jesus was referred to as the Son of God (Matthew 16:16-18). This is an admission to the Divine nature of Jesus. (For a further detailed study of the Divine nature, the writer refers you to the preceding chapter.)

The question comes to mind, "How is it possible for there to be a dual nature?" This is a question that the Bible does not attempt to answer. The Bible never attempts to reconcile Jesus' Deity with His Humanity, and neither should we. To try to reconcile something the Bible doesn't is foolish. Ours is to accept it!

The Purpose of the Incarnation:

What is the purpose of the Incarnation? Why did God become incarnate and live on the earth? What is the reason for such an act of Divine grace?

Professor William Barclay of Glasgow University observed,

To Paul the Incarnation was in the most literal sense an act of God. It is the love of God which is for any man (Romans 8:3). It is the love of God which is in Jesus Christ our Lord (Romans 8:39). It was God who was in Christ reconciling the world unto Himself (II Corinthians 5:19). That gift is an unspeakable gift (II Corinthians 9:15). Before such an act of love, in fact of such a splendor of generosity, there is nothing left for man but silent and grateful adoration. The Incarnation in its essence is an act of God on behalf of man.[4]

There is a purpose behind this Divine act of grace. There is a reason for God sending His only son into the world (John 3:16). This purpose is found in the following:

(1) To reveal God to Man (John 1:14,18). Jesus came to this world to show man what God was like. In Christ, God is revealed (John 14:9). A mediator is necessary; and to reveal God, he must be both Divine and human. This is true of the Christ (I Timothy 2:5-6).

(2) To atone for sin (Hebrews 2:6-10). Jesus was made "a little lower than the angels..." and suffered death that He might "taste death for every man" (Hebrews 2:9). Only by dying such a death could Christ qualify as a Saviour (Hebrews 2:10; II Corinthians 8:9). As a Divine being (spirit), Jesus could not die. To die, He must become a human being, for only human beings are subject to death! And Jesus had to die to atone for the sins of the world. Jesus was put to death in the flesh!

(3) To identify Himself completely with man (Hebrews 2:11-13). This Scripture states, "For both he that sanctifieth [i.e., Jesus] and they that are sanctified [i.e., mankind] are all one [i.e., united]: for which cause he is not ashamed to call them brethren." Jesus wasn't ashamed to condescend to man's level and be recognized, and to recognize man as "brethren." This was necessary, that He might mediate for us adequately. Becoming a man, Jesus knows

how I feel when I am lonely, sad, despondent, and when I suffer.
(4) To destroy the works of Satan (Hebrews 2:14; I John 3:8). Jesus came to earth to "destroy the works of the devil." He became manifest for that very purpose. Satan was king of the earth. He must be dethroned and shorn of his power. People must be delivered from his clutches, and the way for Jesus to do this was to become as a man and offer Himself as the sacrifice for our sins.
(5) To conquer death (Hebrews 2:14-16). Jesus became flesh to deliver men from death and its fear. Death could be conquered only by submitting to it and then overcoming it by a resurrection. Jesus said, "because I live, ye shall live also" (John 14:19).
(6) To qualify as man's High Priest (Hebrews 2:17-18). Jesus could not properly represent us in heaven if He had never been on earth to experience our life. He must, through human suffering, learn sympathy for man. Since he was "tempted in all points like as we are," He is therefore a "merciful and faithful High Priest." By being this, He is able to "succor [help, aid] those that are tempted." Therefore, we are encouraged to pray (Hebrews 4:15-16).
(7) **To set an example of righteous living (I Peter 2:21).** In order to do this, Christ came to the earth. He must demonstrate by His earthly life the possibility of righteous living.

The patriarchs and prophets were not sufficient to be our examples. A perfect life had to be lived in order that a sinless example might be set. Christ, and Christ alone, could do this.

Conclusion:

Man was in a situation from which he could not free himself; he was dominated by sin and was helpless and hopelessly lost, and separated from God. Christ came to the earth to break through this hopelessness and provide for man a way of escape. Professor Barclay summarizes,

What is true is that man was hopelessly and helplessly involved in sin, and that Christ liberated him from that tragic and impotent situation. Through Jesus Christ, man the sinner becomes potentially man the righteous. [5]

Knowing this, we give the praise to Jesus recorded in Revelation 5:9, "Worthy are thou to take the book, and to open the seals thereof: for thou wast slain, and didst purchase unto God with thy blood men of every tribe, and tongue, and people, and nation."

QUESTIONS FOR DISCUSSION

1. Define what is meant by the word "Incarnation."
2. Discuss John 1:14 in light of the definition just given.
3. How does the Incarnation relate to salvation? Discuss.
4. What does the Virgin Birth have to do with the Incarnation?
5. Is a belief in the Incarnation important? Why or why not?
6. Read and discuss I John 4:2-3.
7. What is the result of denying Jesus being manifested in the flesh?
8. Discuss how the Scriptures gave testimony to the Incarnation.
9. Can man fully understand the Incarnation of Jesus?
10. Discuss what was involved in Jesus becoming man.
11. List and discuss the purposes of the Incarnation.

FOOTNOTES

[1] Emery H. Bancroft, *Christian Theology* (Grand Rapids, MI: Zondervan Publishing Co.), p. 85.

[2] Loraine Boettner, *Studies In Theology* (Philadelphia: The Presbyterian Reformed Company), p. 207.

[3] Boettner, p. 203.

[4] William Barclay, *The Mind of St. Paul* (New York: Harper & Row Publishers), p. 60.

[5] Ibid., p.

Chapter Ten
THE RESURRECTION OF CHRIST

John records some of the saddest words that have ever fallen from human lips; he records the Jews as crying, "Crucify him, crucify him" (John 19:6). Then in verse 18 of this same chapter, John records the fulfilling of their wish, "...they crucified Him..." Thus, as Jesus had predicted, the son of God was put to death (cf. John 12:31-34; Luke 24:26). The Lamb of God, which was to take away the sins of the world (John 1:29) had now been slain. At this point, we must be careful to point out that Christ's Deity did not die on the cross. Peter said, "For Christ also died for sins once for all...having been put to **death** in the **flesh** but made alive in the spirit" (I Peter 3:18). The fleshly tabernacle died (Philippians 2:5-8), as Christ committed His Spirit to the Father (Luke 23:46). "And so they took the body of Jesus and bound it in linen wrappings with spices, as the burial custom of the Jews" (John 19:40). What now? The one who had claimed to be from God, and had performed many mighty works (miracles) to support these claims, was now in the grave. There was just one thing left to wait for; that was the promise of the Resurrection.

Christianity is the only religion that bases its claim to acceptance upon the resurrection of its founder. For any other religion to base its claim on such a doctrine would be to court failure. The foundation on which the entire doctrine of Christianity is based on the **fact** of the Resurrection of Jesus Christ from the dead. The extreme importance of this teaching is seen in the part that it played in the preaching of the Apostles. The apostle Paul aptly stated, "...if Christ be not risen, ye are yet in your sins" (I Corinthians 15:14) and "if Christ be not risen, then is our preaching vain, and your faith is also vain" (I Corinthians 15:7). Since our life is one of faith (II Corinthians 5:7), we need to be sure of the foundation on which our faith rests, Jesus Christ (I Corinthians 3:11).

The Conclusive Sign of Christ's Deity:

The resurrection of Jesus Christ from the dead is the conclusive proof of His claims to Deity. There are some who believe that when He healed the sick, cured lepers, raised the dead, and made the blind to see and the lame to walk, He was conclusively, by these acts, proving His Deity. True, these were proofs of His claims, but they were not the final proofs (read John, chapter 6). The miracles that Jesus did were signs to others that He was from God (cf. John 3:1-10), but they were not the only conclusive signs or proofs of His Deity. Moses, Joshua, Elijah, Elisha, Peter, and Paul all performed miracles by the power of God, as Christ did. The miracles that Jesus did were intended to prove His Deity, because He claimed to be the Son of God, a claim the Jews understood to mean equal with God (John 14:6-14; 8:37-59; 5:18). When Jesus raised Lazarus from the grave, it brought glory to God and made a contribution toward proving His Deity (John 11:4,23-54), but even this great event is not the conclusive proof.

Therefore, as a general rule, let us remember that miracles prove that one is from God (like Moses, Joshua, etc.). They did that for the apostles as they did for Christ. The difference, as far as purpose is concerned, lies in the claims behind the miracles. Christ claimed to be the Son of God, thus Divine. Therefore, His miracles all contributed to proving His claim to Deity. The Apostles worked miracles, not to prove that they were Divine, but to support their claims as messengers from God who had seen the resurrected Christ (I Corinthians 15:1-4, etc.). The conclusive sign that proved the ultimate truthfulness of Jesus' claim was His resurrection from the dead. This is what He, Himself, expressly taught.

Jesus referred to Jonah's three days and nights in the belly of the whale as a sign of His resurrection (Matthew 12:39,40). According to Jesus, there was to be a conclusive sign given to them to prove His claims, and ultimately His Deity. That sign was after being three days and nights in the heart of the earth, He would come forth as Jonah had come forth from the belly of the great fish. Thus, when Jesus was raised from the dead, He was "declared to be the son of God with power" (Romans 1:4, cf. Matthew 28:18-20). The signs spoken of in John 20:30-31, which included the resurrection, are said to be recorded to cause us to believe in Christ as the Son of God. Therefore, when they were being performed, they were for this purpose also (all of them). Thomas said, after seeing the resurrected Christ, "My Lord and my God" (John 20:28).

A Main Event in Man's History:

So powerful was the Resurrection of Christ from the dead that it stands as a main event in man's history. Heinrich Ewald made this observation,

Nothing stands more historically certain than that Jesus rose from the dead and appeared again to His followers, or than that their seeing Him thus again was the beginning of a higher faith, and of all their Christian work in the world. It is equally certain that they thus saw Him, not as a common man, or as a shade or ghost risen from the grave; but as the One Son of God already more than man, alike in nature and power; and that all who thus beheld Him, recognized at once and instinctively His unique Divine dignity, and firmly believed in it thenceforth.

The Historical Reality:

The historical reality of the Resurrection cannot be denied even by the skeptics. Guignebert, in his book entitled *Jesus,* vehemently repudiates all the miracles of the New Testament. But towards the end of the book, he admits the following:

There would have been no Christianity if the belief in the Resurrection had not been founded and systematized...The whole of the soteriology [defined: that which pertains to a study of salvation—EPM] and the essential teaching of Christianity rests on the belief of the Resurrection, and on the first page of any account of Christian dogma might be written as a motto Paul's declaration: "And if Christ be not risen, then is our preaching vain, and your faith is also vain." From the strictly historical point of view, the importance of the belief in the Resurrection is scarcely less...By means of that belief, faith in Jesus and His mission become the fundamental element of a new religion which, after separating from, became the opponent of Judaism and set out to conquer the world.

Wilbur Smith states,

The resurrection is either a fact in itself or it is a fiction—it matters not whether designed or undesigned—on which no belief can be founded. If the Resurrection be not true, then death still remains the great conqueror. [1]

Argument for a Single Miracle

We shall endeavor, then, to argue for a single miracle in the Bible—**the Resurrection of Christ!** If this can be shown to be true, then other miracles will be easy. If not, the rest will not matter. There are several witnesses to the Resurrection. We could give reference to the written testimony of six men—Matthew, Mark, Luke, John, Peter, and Paul; or give reference to the appearances of Jesus between the time of His resurrection and the ascension some forty days later.

Witnesses to the Resurrection:

Perhaps for the best results we should list the appearances of Jesus following His resurrection. They are:

(1) To certain women as they returned from the sepulchre, after having seen the angel who told them Christ had risen (Matthew 28:9-11).

(2) To Mary Magdalene at the sepulchre (Mark 16:9-11; John 20:11-18).

(3) To the apostle Peter, before the evening of the day.

(4) To the two disciples, Cleopas and another, on the way to Emmaus, on the afternoon of the Resurrection (Mark 16:12-13; Luke 24:36-40).

(5) To the ten apostles, Thomas being absent (Mark 16:14-18; Luke

24:36-40; John 20:19-23; I Corinthians 15:50).
(6) One week later, to all the eleven apostles, probably in the same place as the preceding appearance (John 20:26-28).
(7) To several disciples at the sea of Galilee, while they were fishing (John 21:21-23).
(8) To the Apostles, and above five hundred brethren, at once, on an appointed mountain in Galilee (Matthew 28:16-20; I Corinthians 15:6).
(9) To James, under circumstances of which we have no information (I Corinthians 15:7).
(10) To the Apostles at Jerusalem, immediately before the Ascension on the Mount of Olives (Mark 16:19; Luke 24:50-52; Acts 1:3-8).

Thus the preceding gives evidence for the Resurrection of Jesus. It is, however, beyond this point that we wish to present further testimony for the resurrection. Perhaps it would be best to state our intention in the form of two propositions:
(1) The open and empty tomb gives evidence that Jesus of Nazareth was raised from the dead; and
(2) The completed work of the Holy Spirit among the Apostles as promised by Christ is proof of the Resurrection of Christ.

The Open and Empty Tomb:

All four Gospels record the burial of the Lord in the tomb of Joseph of Arimathaea following His crucifixion and death on the cross. At this time, one could wonder how the disciples must have felt. Jesus had told them of His death and that He would be raised on the third day (Matthew 12:39-40; Mark 15:42-47). Even the Old Testament Scriptures had testified that the Messiah was to die (cf. Psalm 16:9-10 as quoted by Peter in Acts 2:26-27). But the disciples did not believe that this would happen (cf. Matthew 16:21-22).

Many people have tried to explain away Jesus' death on the cross. Essentially they deny the bodily resurrection of Christ. They believe in a resurrection, but not a bodily resurrection.

They explain His death and resurrection as being merely the two sides of the one experience: in His death He passed out of His physical life, and in his resurrection He passed into His spiritual life. Thus His death and resurrection are declared to be simultaneous events. [5] His appearances after the Resurrection are explained as those of His spirit or as subjective hallucinations. People who accept these theories have problems and must give satisfactory and logical explanation before this writer can change his view of the bodily resurrection.

This much is fact: there was a body on the cross, which body was taken down from the cross and placed in the tomb of Joseph of Arimathaea. Concerning this Wilbur Smith states,

We know more about the burial of the Lord Jesus than we know of the burial of any single character in all of ancient history. We know infinitely more about His burial than we do the burial of any Old Testament character, or any king of Babylon, Pharaoh of Egypt, any philosopher of Greece, or triumphant Caesar. We know who took His body from the Cross; we know something of the wrapping of the body in the spices, and burial clothes; we know the very tomb in which this body was placed, the name of the man who owned it, Joseph, of a town known as Arimathaea. We know even where this tomb was located, in a garden nigh to the place where He was crucified, outside the city walls. We know minute details concerning events immediately subsequent to our Lord's entombment, that a stone was sealed and that, by wish of the Jews, Roman guards were set before the tomb to prevent the body being stolen.

Jesus' body was prepared and placed in a tomb. Yet on Sunday morning, the tomb was found open and empty! With this fact at hand, we must find either a logical explanation as to where the body of Jesus was or accept the
resurrection. The disciples found the tomb empty and, remembering His words, they accepted the Resurrection.

Some have tried to reason away what happened to the body of Jesus. They say that Christ never did really die. He merely swooned away into a trance and, after being removed from the cross, His disciples took Him away to the tomb and treated Him for His wounds and, after this, He appeared to be resurrected from the dead.[5] But, believing this provides greater problems than a belief in the Resurrection. For instance, if Jesus was not really dead but merely swooned away, why didn't the soldiers break His legs as was their custom? (cf. John 19:31-37.) Or, how did Jesus survive the spear thrust into His side? The fact is, He could not. **He died!** Just as the scripture says He did (John 19:33).

Yet remember, on Sunday morning following the crucifixion, the tomb was **open** and **empty.**

No man has ever written, pro or con, on the subject of Christ's resurrection, without finding himself compelled to face this problem of Joseph's empty tomb. That the tomb was empty on Sunday morning is recognized by everyone, no matter how radical a critic he may be; however anti-supernatural in all his personal convictions, he never dares to say that the body was still resting in that tomb.

Luke tells us that when the three women came to the tomb of Jesus, the stone was rolled away and the tomb was open (Luke 24:2). John tells us that Mary Magdalene ran back from the tomb and told Simon Peter and the disciple whom Jesus loved and they ran to the tomb, entered and found it empty (John 20:1-9). The question is then placed on us, "How did the tomb become empty?" In order to satisfy themselves, some people have sought to explain the empty tomb in the following ways:

(1) **Friends took the body**—Some say that friends took the body of Jesus. Let us take a moment and examine this. According to Matthew's account, Pilate gave the chief priests and Pharisees permission to make the tomb secure and to place a guard at the

opening (Matthew 27:62-66). In order for friends of Jesus to remove the body, they had to get by the Roman guards and remove the large stone. But why should they do so? They were still grieving over their Lord's death. Luke records that they were bringing spices to the tomb to prepare His body (Luke 24:1-2). Does this sound like a group of people who were trying to steal the body of Jesus from the tomb?

(2) **Enemies stole the body**—Another says the enemies of Jesus stole His body. [11] This really can be answered by asking one question. If the enemies of Jesus stole the body, why did they not produce His body when the disciples were preaching that He was raised from the dead? If they wanted to put an end to the resurrection story, all they had to do was to produce the body of Jesus and Christianity would have been shown to be a fraud. In answer to this question, J. N. D. Anderson stated, "To me there's only one answer: They couldn't, because they didn't know where the body was!" [12]

(3) **The grave clothes**—The grave clothes in which Jesus was wrapped after His death also need to be accounted for. It is a matter of history that they were on the inside of the tomb. John records for us that Peter and the disciple whom Jesus loved ran into the tomb and found the linen clothes lying and the napkin that was upon his head, not lying with the linen clothes, but rolled up in a place by itself (John 20:4-7).

If the friends or enemies of Jesus were removing the body from the tomb, why would they take the time to remove the linen and napkin? It just doesn't make sense that they would take the time to do such a thing. William Barclay, professor of New Testament at Glasgow University and renowned as a scholar of New Testament Greek, insists that the Greek text actually means that the clothes were "lying in their folds." That is, they were in a cocoon-type shell, as if Jesus had simply passed through them without disturbance.

The napkin around Jesus was bound around him in the same way that it was bound around Lazarus (John 11:44-45; 19:40). He was bound hand and foot. Why would anyone take the time to unwrap him and leave the linen and napkin in such ordered positions?

In light of the foregoing evidence, we conclude that Jesus Christ was raised from the dead and challenge the unbeliever to come up with a better answer to the **open** and **empty** tomb.

The Complete Work of the Holy Spirit Among the Apostles:

This can, if used properly, be one of the strongest arguments for the Resurrection of Christ that can be found. For clarification, let's repeat the proposition: **The completed work of the Holy Spirit among the Apostles as promised by Christ is proof of the Resurrection.**

To begin this testimony, we must first observe the mission of the Holy Spirit as presented by Jesus. In John 14:25-26, the scriptures read,

These things have I spoken unto you, while yet abiding with you. But the Comforter, even the Holy Spirit, whom the Father will send in my name, he shall teach you all things, and bring to your remembrance all that I have said unto you.

In John 16:12-13, Jesus states,

I have many things to say unto you, but ye cannot bear them now. Howbeit when he, the Spirit of truth, is come, he shall guide you into all truth; for he shall not speak from himself; but what things soever he shall hear, these shall he speak; and he shall declare unto you the things that are to come.

Jesus promised unto the Apostles a supernatural power and guidance to be with them—the Holy Spirit. Their guidance was to be to the extent that they would be taught all things, would remember all things, and would be declared things that were at that time yet to come.

However, the mission of the Holy Spirit in the lives of the Apostles was dependent upon Christ's return to the Father. In John 16:7, Jesus said, Nevertheless, I tell you the truth: It is expedient for you that I go away; for **if I go not away, the Comforter will not come unto you: but if I go, I will send him unto you.**

During the earthly ministry of Christ, and even prior to Pentecost, the Apostles had a nationalistic concept of the Messiah. On one occasion, Peter said that he would not allow his Master to suffer and die. He would fight for him (cf. Matthew 16:21-28). Peter's concept of the Messiah and His kingdom was entirely earthly—nationalistic (Jewish).

James and John, the sons of Zebedee, had the same concept when they came to Jesus and asked permission to sit one on the right hand and the other on his left (cf. Mark 10:35-38). On the day of Jesus' ascension back to heaven, the disciples' concept of the kingdom was still national—earthly. This is seen in the question they ask, "Lord, dost thou at **this time** restore the kingdom to Israel?" (cf. Acts 1:6.) So, right up until the time of Jesus' return to the Father, the disciples of the Lord were looking for an earthly (nationalistic) kingdom.

However, notice the lives of the Apostles **after** the first Pentecost following the resurrection and you see something different. They testified that Christ had been raised from the dead and that they were witnesses that He actually lived again! (cf. Acts 2:32; 3:14-15; 10:39-41; et al.) They were changed men, there's no doubt about it! Something happened! They are not the same men that once asked to sit on His right and left hand. They are different. How can we explain this change in the lives of the Apostles? And what could account for the astonishing change in these men in so short a time? What changed the concept of the Apostles from a nationalistic concept to a spiritual concept of preaching Christ crucified? What forces would be required to combine themselves together to produce such a drastic radical change? Could such a change occur by natural forces and affect the disciples in such a short time? (Remember: From the ascension to Pentecost was ten days.) How is it possible that in such a short period of time the disciples changed their concept of the kingdom? To change a concept demands education, and education demands time. Yet, in ten days' time the Apostles' concept of the kingdom is changed! What's the answer?

The only answer that can be given that is consistent with Jesus' teaching and apostolic claims is that the Apostles must have received Divine guidance as Jesus said they would (cf. passages already referred to—John 14:25-26; John 16:12-13). The fact that the Apostles' concept and knowledge of Christ's Kingdom was changed from national to spiritual, from Judaistic to universal, from fearfulness to boldness, within a matter of days, argues strongly for the coming of the Holy Spirit upon these disciples and superimposing His knowledge upon them, and thus effecting their change in a miraculous way as Jesus promised would happen. A slight look at their claims for possession of the Spirit shows even further evidence of fulfillment (cf. I Corinthians 2:12-13).

But remember, Jesus had been betrayed, tried, crucified, died on Golgotha's cross and was buried in a tomb (Matthew 26:27-47,66; Mark 14:43-15:47; Luke 22:47-23:56; John 18:1-19:42). Since Jesus had died and was buried and yet stated that the coming of the Spirit was dependent upon His returning to the Father in Heaven, we must conclude that Jesus was raised from the dead in order to ascend to the Father and send the Holy Spirit as He stated He would do (John 16:7,12-13).

This miraculous change wrought in the Apostles can only be explained by the supernatural power given them by the presence of the Holy Spirit, but the Spirit could only be given to them when Jesus returned to the Father. Thus, **the testimony given by the completed work of the Holy Spirit in the lives of the Apostles is that Jesus was** raised from the dead. He returned to the Father in Heaven, and sent the Holy Spirit to them.

The Holy Spirit Raised Jesus:

In Romans, chapter eight, Paul encourages Christians to live a godly life. In doing this, he reminds them of their hope, which is based upon the work of the Holy Spirit. He said,

But if the Spirit of Him that raised up Jesus from the dead dwelleth in you, he that raised up Christ from the dead shall give life also to your mortal bodies through his Spirit that dwelleth in you (Romans 8:11).

Therefore, from the Incarnation to the ascension of Christ, we see the cooperative work of three Persons within the One Divine Being about the plan to redeem fallen man. Our hope is that one day the same Spirit will resurrect our mortal bodies.

Conclusion:

We conclude by noticing, "...if Christ be not risen, ye are yet in your sins" **(I** Corinthians **15:14).** But, **He has been raised! O, joyous hope!** May we go forth and share it with others (Mark **16:15-16).**

QUESTIONS FOR DISCUSSION

1. Why is a belief in the Resurrection important?
2. How did Jesus say He would show His Deity? To what event in days gone by did He refer to parallel this event?
3. Can the resurrection of Christ be shown to be historical? Discuss.
4. Why is an argument for this single miracle (the Resurrection) so important?
5. List and discuss the witnesses to the Resurrection.
6. What problem does the skeptic run into regarding the Resurrection?
7. What is meant by "Jesus didn't die but 'swooned away' "?
8. Answer the following charges for the empty tomb:
    a. Friends took His body.

b. Enemies took His body.

9. Discuss the Grave Clothes and their position in the tomb.

10. Present and discuss **(carefully)** the argument for the Resurrection from the completed work of the Holy Spirit in the lives of the Apostles.

FOOTNOTES

[1] Heinrich Ewald, as quoted by Cunningham Geike, *The Life and Words of Christ* (London: Cassell and Company, no date), p. 7221.

[2] Ch. Guingenebert, as quoted by Wilbur Smith, *The Supernaturalness of Christ* (Boston, MA: W. A. Wilde Co., 1941), p. 189.

[3] Wilbur Smith, *The Supernaturalness of Christ* (W. A. Wilde Co., 1941), p. 195.

[4] Matthew 27:57-61; Mark 15:42-47; Luke 23:50-56; John 19:38-42.

[5] Henry C. Theissen, *Lectures In Systematic Theology* (Grand Rapids, MI: Wm. B. Eerdman Pub. Co., 1971), p. 333.

[6] One of these problems is Jesus' appearance to Thomas, allowing him to see and feel him (John 20:26-29).

[7] Wilbur Smith, *Therefore Stand* (Boston, MA: W. A. Wilde Co., 1945), p. 371.

[8] Ibid., p. 209.

[9] Ibid., p. 373-374.

[10] J. W. McGarvey, *Evidences of Christianity—Part III* (Nashville, TN: Gospel Advocate Co., 1964), p. 133.

[11] Smith, p. 211.

[12] J. N. D. Anderson, "The Resurrection of Jesus Christ," *Christianity Today* (March 29, 1968), Vol. 13, p. 6.

[13] As referred to by Edward C. Wharton, "The Resurrection of Jesus Christ—Historical or Mythological?" (unpublished paper), p. 27.

Chapter Eleven
THE HOLY SPIRIT: ATTRIBUTES

Introduction

As we begin this chapter, we enter into a study that has been greatly theorized by the religious world. Speculation has had its toll among religious leaders for centuries concerning the Holy Spirit. It is not our desire to present and answer all that has been written or stated about the Biblical Doctrine of the Holy Spirit.

Much confusion is found even today in the religious world concerning the Holy Spirit. Because of the confusion, many preachers fail to preach on the subject and, for fear of antagonistic criticism, many will not even write about it. Some people teach that the Holy Spirit is a mere substance or fluid. Others refer to the Spirit as a mere influence or power. And others believe the Holy Spirit is a mysterious force that operates on the heart of man to bring about repentance and salvation. Much emphasis is being given today to the ministry of the Holy Spirit. However, we feel that anytime a movement gives more emphasis to the Spirit than it does to Christ, and is more concerned with Pentecost than it is with Calvary, that movement is biblically **unbalanced.**

It is admitted here that there is a deep mystery regarding the doctrine of the Holy Spirit. However, this is true of the doctrine of the entire Godhead. The fact that there are some things mysterious or that there has been wrong teaching done in the past about it doesn't mean we should exclude a study of that subject today.

Let it be stated in the beginning that what man knows about the Spirit of God can **only** come by way of Revelation **(the Bible).** For without Revelation we could know nothing concerning the working of the Holy Spirit.

We shall limit ourselves, therefore, to what the Bible says about the Holy Spirit and leave speculation to others.

The Personality of the Holy Spirit:

The question is often asked, "Who is the Holy Spirit?" The answer is very simple. The Holy Spirit is the third person of the Godhead. However, the explanation of such an answer is not quite so simple. The Holy Spirit is not a mere force or influence, nor is the Spirit to be referred to as an "it." The Holy Spirit is a person. We fall into error when we refer to the Holy Spirit as an "It," as if He were some impersonal type of force.

The Holy Spirit is ascribed human feelings, attributes, conduct, and characteristics. It might be objected by some that the Bible refers to the Spirit in an impersonal way. True, the Hebrew **(ruach)** and the Greek **(pneuma)** words translated "Spirit" are neuter words and originally meant "wind." In the King James Version, the idea of an impersonal being is found by some in such passages as Romans 8:16, "The Spirit itself beareth witness with our spirit, that we are children of God." However, the following should help to establish in our minds that the Spirit is a person.

(1) **Contrary to the neuter usage, the masculine pronoun "He" (in the English texts) is used twelve times in John 16:7,8,13,14. The Spirit is constantly referred to as "He" or "Him."** Jesus said, "But when **He,** the Comforter, is come, whom I will send unto you from the Father, even the Spirit of truth, which proceedeth from the Father, **He** shall testify of me" (John 15:26). In Acts 13:2, Luke records, "As they ministered to the Lord, and fasted, the Holy Spirit said, Separate me Barnabas and Saul for the work whereunto I have called them." The American Standard Version and the Revised Standard Version correctly render Romans 8:16 as "the Spirit Himself."

(2) The personal attribute of speaking is ascribed to the Spirit—

(a) I Timothy 4:1 states, "The Spirit speaketh expressly...";

(b) Acts 8:29, "And the Spirit said..."; and (c) Acts 10:19, "And while Peter thought on the vision, the Spirit **said** unto him..."

(3) **The personal attribute of teaching** is ascribed to the Spirit. John 14:26, "But the Comforter, even the Holy Spirit, whom the Father will send in my name, he [i.e., the Spirit] shall **teach** you all things."

(4) **The personal attribute of a mind** is ascribed to the Holy Spirit. Romans 8:27 states, "And he that searcheth the hearts knoweth what is the **mind** of the Spirit."

(5) **The personal attribute of love** is ascribed to the Holy Spirit. Paul pleads, "Now I beseech you, brethren, by our Lord Jesus Christ, and by the **love** of the Spirit, that ye strive together with me in your prayers to God for me" (Romans 15:30).

(6) The personal attribute of searching is ascribed to the Holy Spirit.

In I Corinthians 2:10, scripture states, "But unto us God revealed them through the Spirit, for the Spirit **searcheth** all things, yea, the deep things of God."

The Characteristics of the Holy Spirit:

Not only does the Bible present the personality of the Holy Spirit, but the Bible also ascribes to the Holy Spirit characteristics of a person. This is found in the following:

(1) **The Spirit can be grieved.** Ephesians **4:30,** "And **grieve** not the Holy Spirit..." One can grieve the Holy Spirit when we speak unkind words, think impure thoughts, and perform selfish deeds. The same idea is expressed in Isaiah **63:10.** The Spirit is not a mere force but is capable of feeling.

(2) **The Spirit can be lied to.** In Acts **5:3,** Ananias lied to the Holy Spirit and in Acts **5:9,** his wife, Sapphira, lied to the Spirit. Understood in this sin is a sin against the very nature of the Spirit, who is the "Spirit of Truth."

(3) **The Spirit can be resisted.** In Acts **7:51,** Stephen accused the Jews of "resisting the Holy Spirit." The word "resist" here means "to strive against." [1] To resist the Spirit today would be to resist

what He says. Men today resist the Words of the Spirit when they strive against what the Bible teaches.

(4) **The Spirit can be despised.** Hebrews **10:29** reads, "Of how much sorer punishment, think ye, shall he be judged worthy, who hath trodden under foot the Son of God, and hath counted the blood of the covenant wherewith he was sanctified an unholy thing, and hath done **despite** unto the Spirit of Grace?" The word **despite** means "to use wanton insult towards."[2] These men were despising the Spirit of Grace by rejecting all the good that the Spirit had done for them.

(5) **The Spirit can be blasphemed.** In Matthew 12:31, Jesus says, "Therefore I say unto you, every sin and blasphemy shall be forgiven unto men, but the blasphemy against the Holy Spirit shall not be forgiven." H. Leo Boles says that the blasphemy against the Holy Spirit "...is a malignant, persistent, willful rejection of the Holy Spirit linked with an imputing to the Holy Spirit hellish purposes against reason and conclusive evidence." [3]

The Holy Spirit—A Divine Person:

The Bible also teaches that the Holy Spirit is a Divine Person. We have seen that the Spirit is a person by looking at the personality and characteristics of the Spirit. Here we wish to see that the Spirit is not only a person but, by virtue of the attributes ascribed to Him, He is a Divine Person:

(1) **The Spirit is Eternal.** "How much more shall the blood of Christ, who through the eternal Spirit offered himself without blemish unto God, cleanse your conscience from dead works to serve the living God?" (Hebrews 9:14).

(2) **The Spirit is Omnipresent (everywhere).** David declared, "Whither shall I go from thy Spirit? Or whither shall I flee from thy presence? If I ascend up into heaven, thou art there: If I make my bed in Sheol, behold, thou art there. If I take the wings of the morning, and dwell in the uttermost parts of the sea; even there

shall thy hand lead me, and thy right hand shall hold me" (Psalm 139:7-10).

(3) **The Spirit is Omnipotent (all powerful).** Paul "worked through mighty signs and wonders, by the power of the Spirit of God" (Romans 15:19). Micah proclaimed, "But as for me, I am full of power by the Spirit of Jehovah, and of judgment and of might, to declare unto Jacob his transgression, and to Israel his sin" (Micah 3:8). The virgin birth of our Lord was by the power of the Holy Spirit (Luke 1:35).

(4) **The Spirit is Omniscient (all knowing).** "Who hath directed the Spirit of the Lord, or being his counsellor hath taught him? With whom he took counsel, and who instructed him, and taught him in the faith of judgment, and taught him knowledge, and showed to him the way of understanding?" (Isaiah 40:13-14). Paul declared that the Spirit knew all things and revealed them to him. **(Read carefully** I Corinthians 2:1-11.)

The Holy Spirit—Divine Works:

The Holy Spirit is spoken of as God (cf. Acts 5:3-4; I Corinthians 3:16, 6:19, 12:4-6), and works which only God can perform are attributed to him:

(1) **Creation**—The Holy Spirit had a part in the creation of the world. This is taught by such passages as Genesis 1:2; Job 26:13, 33:4.

(2) **Regeneration**—The Spirit also has a part in the regeneration of man according to John 3:5.

(3) **Resurrection**—The Spirit also has a part in the resurrection. Paul stated in Romans 8:11, "But if the Spirit of him that raised up Jesus from the dead dwelleth in you, he that raised up Christ Jesus from the dead shall give life also to your mortal bodies through his Spirit that dwelleth in you."

(4) **Miracles**—The Spirit gave the power to perform miracles (cf. I Corinthians 12:9,11). Men performed miracles only by the power

from the Spirit of God. Miracles that were performed were manifested by such acts as healing the sick, making the blind to see, the lame to walk, and the dumb to talk, speaking in tongues, prophesying, etc., but all these miracles were done by the power of the Spirit of God.

(5) **Revelation**—The Spirit gave revelation from God. Such was the case for Joseph in regard to Pharaoh's dream (Genesis 41:16,38); and Paul stated that the gospel that he preached was received by way of revelation (Galatians 1:11-12).

(6) **Inspiration**—The Holy Spirit inspired the writers of the Old and New Testaments, guiding them as they wrote so we could have the infallible Word of God (II Peter 1:21; II Timothy 3:16-17).

(7) **Interceding**—The Spirit of God works in behalf of the Christian (Romans 8:26).

(8) **Sanctifying**—The Spirit of God sanctifies (sets apart) obedient man unto God (II Thessalonians 2:13).

(9) **Comforting**—The Holy Spirit was given to the Apostles as a Comforter (John 14:16). The work of comforting was no doubt given to strengthen them in their afflictions and persecutions which they were to endure as a result of living for Christ.

(10) **Reproving/Convicting**—The Holy Spirit convicts the world in respect of sin, and of righteousness, and of judgment to come (John **16:8).**

"These attributes and works which are ascribed to the Holy Spirit could only belong to a person. Hence, He is, like God and Christ, an individual person. Throughout the Scriptures from their beginning to their end we see God, Christ, and the Holy Spirit as Divine Beings, living, acting, influencing, blessing, reconciling, transforming, loving, and glorifying. The Holy Spirit is thus not seen as a thing, but as a glorious person—**The Holy Spirit**".[4]

The Holy Spirit—Member of the Godhead:

We have already established that the Spirit is Divine by looking at the Divine works that He performs. Here we wish to give further evidence to the Deity of the Spirit by showing that scripture refers to Him as a member of the Godhead, equal in substance and rank with God the Father and God the Son—He is God the Holy Spirit.

(1) The Holy Spirit is equated with the Jehovah of the Old Testament. **In several New Testament passages that ascribe works to the Holy Spirit, the Old Testament text says that Jehovah did it. Paul cites a passages in Acts 28:25-27, and says that the Holy Spirit speaks through Isaiah. But in Isaiah 6:9-10, the Old Testament text says Jehovah spoke it.**

(2) The Holy Spirit is mentioned in unity with the Godhead. There are several passages where this is seen:

(a) At the baptism of Jesus, all three are mentioned (Mark 1:9-11; Matthew 3:13-17).

(b) Jesus spoke of the Comforter, the Father, and Himself in John 15:26.

(c) Paul mentions the Lord Jesus Christ, the Spirit, and God in Romans 15:30.

(d) Jesus said we are to baptize in the name of the Father, Son, and the Holy Spirit (Matthew 28:18-20).

(e) Paul gives in his salutation the Lord Jesus Christ, God, and the Holy Spirit (II Corinthians 13:14).

(f) Peter addresses his first epistle to the dispersion "according to the foreknowledge of God, in sanctification of the Spirit, unto obedience and sprinkling of the blood of the Lord Jesus Christ" (1 Peter 1:2).

(g) In Ephesians 4:4-6, the scripture states that there is One Lord, One Spirit, and One God and Father of all.

These passages clearly show that the Holy Spirit is mentioned in connection with the Godhead. Add to this the fact that the word translated "God" in the Bible is a word that is plural in form, and you have a good weight of evidence for showing that the Spirit is a member of the Godhead.

(3) **The Holy Spirit is called "God" in the Bible.** In Acts 5:3-4, Ananias is accused of lying to the Holy Spirit, and then it is stated, "thou hast not lied unto men, but unto God."

(4) The Holy Spirit can be seen to be Divine by the names given to Him in the Scripture. These are:

(a) The Spirit of God (Genesis 1:2; Matthew 3:16).
(b) Spirit of the Lord (Luke 4:18).
(c) Spirit of our God (I Corinthians 6:11).
(d) His Spirit (Numbers 11:29).
(e) Spirit of Jehovah (Judges 3:10).
(f) Thy Spirit (Psalms 139:7).
(g) Spirit of the Lord God (Isaiah 61:1).
(h) Spirit of your Father (Matthew 10:20).
(i) Spirit of the living God (II Corinthians 3:3).
(j) My Spirit (Genesis 6:3).
(k) Spirit of Him (Romans 8:11).
(l) Spirit of Truth (John 14:17).

Conclusion:

We have introduced the subject before us of a study of the Holy Spirit. The purpose of this lesson was to see that the Spirit is not a glorified "it" or an impersonal force, but that the Holy Spirit is described in the Bible as a Personal Divine Being who shares equality with the Father and Son as a member of the Godhead. The attributes ascribed to Him in Scripture can only be ascribed to an intelligent personality. Let us therefore exalt Him to His rightful place as a Divine Person and make His work meaningful in our lives.

QUESTIONS FOR DISCUSSION

1. Is the religious world united in its teaching regarding the Holy Spirit? Why not?
2. What are some of the views held by religious people regarding the Holy Spirit? Discuss these.

3. Is a study of the Holy Spirit so difficult and mysterious that we should not study it at all?
4. How long has it been since you have studied in a class the subject of the Holy Spirit of God? What about a sermon preached on the subject?
5. Discuss what is meant by the Personality of the Spirit.
6. List and discuss the characteristics of the Holy Spirit.
7. How would a person do the following today:
a. Grieve the Holy Spirit?
b. Despise the Holy Spirit?
c. Resist the Holy Spirit?
d. Lie to the Holy Spirit?
e. Blaspheme the Holy Spirit?
8. Can it be shown that the Holy Spirit is definitely a Person? How?
9. Show that the Holy Spirit is a Divine Person.
10. List and discuss the Divine Works performed by the Holy Spirit. Does the Holy Spirit do any of these today?
11. From scripture, show that the Holy Spirit is a member of the Godhead.

FOOTNOTS

[1] E. W. Bullinger, *A Critical Lexicon and Concordance to the English and Greek New Testament* (London: Samuel Bagster and Sons Lited, Eighth Edition, 1957), p. 641.

[2] Ibid., p. 220.

[3] H. Leo Boles, *The Holy Spirit* (Nashville, TN: Gospel Advocate Pub. Co., 1942), p. 164.

[4] Garth W. Black, *The Holy Spirit* (Abilene, TX: Biblical Research Press, 1967), p. 6.

Chapter Twelve
THE HOLY SPIRIT IN THE TESTAMENTS
Introduction:

It is the purpose of this chapter to present a study of the Holy Spirit of God as revealed in both the Old and New Testaments. As a person views Divine Revelation, he might possibly conclude that the Holy Spirit does not play a very important part in the Testaments, for Jehovah is presented as the prominent figure of the Old Testament and Jesus is presented in the same manner in the New Testament. However, lest we forget, let it be restated here that the Holy Spirit is the author of both the Old and New Testaments, as He divinely guided the men who wrote them (cf. II Peter 1:20-21; I Corinthians 2:6-16).

The Holy Spirit, however, is mentioned in both Testaments numerous times. In the Old Testament, the Spirit is referred to in 23 out of 39 books and, in the New Testament, He is referred to in every book, with the exception of Philemon and II and III John.

As we continue in this study of the Holy Spirit of God, let us be aware of the fact that we are not studying something that the Bible is silent about but, rather, we are studying a subject about which much is revealed in the Bible.

The Holy Spirit in the Old Testament:

In the Old Testament, the Spirit is referred to by many names. A few of these are:

(1) The Spirit;
(2) The Spirit of God;
(3) The Spirit of Jehovah;
(4) The Spirit of the Lord; and
(5) The Holy Spirit.

The Holy Spirit and One God. Both the Old Testament and the New Testament emphasize the One God. This One God is shown to consist of three persons: Father, Son, and Spirit. The Old Testament shows that God and the Spirit of God are distinct from one another and not to be thought of as identical. This is found in the following:

(1) Isaiah 40:13, "Who hath directed the Spirit of Jehovah, or being his counsellor hath taught him?"

(2) Psalms 139:7, "Whither shall 1 go from thy spirit? Or whither shall I flee from thy presence?"

(3) Isaiah 63:10, "But they rebelled, and grieved his Holy Spirit: therefore **He** [Jehovah] was turned to be their enemy."

(4) Other passages you may wish to look up are: Jeremiah 31:33; Ezekiel 36:27; Genesis 1:2, 6:3; Psalms 51:11; Nehemiah 9:20; Psalms 104:29-35.

Concerning this thought, Garth Black observed,

These passages do not prove that God and the Spirit of God were thought of as distinct beings by the Old Testament writers, but only that the Spirit had activities of His own distinct from God. [1]

The Holy Spirit in Creation. In the creation of the world, the Godhead was present. Usually the work of creation is attributed to God without any special mention of who in the Godhead did what. However, the Bible states that Father, Son, and Spirit each played very important roles in the creation. The Bible says, "In the beginning God **[Elohim—plural] created"** (Genesis 1:1). In this statement, we thus see that the Godhead was present.

God, the Father, planned, purposed, originated, and ruled all things. Jesus, the Word, was the agent of creation (John 1:1-3; Colossians 1:16-18; Hebrews 1:2). The Spirit also played a role in creation. He organized, gave laws, and guides. We see this from:

(1) **Genesis 1:2.** The first account of the Spirit's work in creation is stated, **"and The Spirit of God moved upon the face of the waters."** "The word translated 'moved or brooded' literally means 'to be anxious over, to be tremulous, as with love.' This indicates the Spirit's anxiety to get to work and bring order out of chaos.

Thus, in this, the first mention of the Holy Spirit of God, we already have an indication of the nature of the Holy Spirit and His work. He is the 'order-bringer.' " [2]

(2) Psalm 104:30. "Thou sendest forth thy Spirit, they are created; and thou renewest the face of the ground." According to this, the Spirit played a part in creating this universe. He (the Spirit) brought order out of chaos. The word used in this passage for "created" is the Hebrew word bara. This word is consistently used to mean, not the arranging or assembling of matter already in existence, but implying the original production of matter where there was none before; or, to make something out of nothing.

(3) **Job 26:13. "By his Spirit the heavens are garnished."** The word "garnished" means "to set in order, adorn, or beautify." Thus, the Spirit is said to have "set in order the heavens."

(4) **Job 33:4. "The Spirit of God hath made me, and the breath of the Almighty hath given me life."** This passage concurs with Genesis 1:26, where it states, "And God said, let us make man in our image." God made man and the Spirit made man. The Spirit, then, gave life to man.

The Holy Spirit in the Lives of Old Testament People. The Holy Spirit worked in the lives of people as recorded in the Old Testament. He came upon rulers and kings to help them in their guidance of God's people. The Spirit of God is the source of all supernatural powers and activities which are directed to the foundation, preservation, and development of the Kingdom of God in the midst of a wicked world. As the Spirit worked in the lives of people, we find Him doing the following:

(1) **The Spirit brought God's Word to the people.** II Peter 1:21 says, "For no prophecy ever came by the will of man: but men spake from God, being moved by the Holy Spirit." The phrase "being moved by the Holy Spirit" literally means to be borne along by or guided by the Spirit. Thus, Paul states in II Timothy 3:16, "all

scripture is given by inspiration of God." The word "inspired" means "God-breathed." Hebrews 1:1 says that God spoke unto the Fathers by the prophets.

Many of the prophets claimed they were speaking for God. In Isaiah 61:1, Isaiah said, "The Spirit of the Lord is upon me." And it was said of them, "yet many years didst thou fear with them, and testifiedst against them by the Spirit through thy prophets: yet would they not give ear" (Nehemiah 9:30).

(2) **The Spirit revealed God's Will.** Of this, we refer to such incidents as the Spirit helping Joseph to reveal Pharaoh's dream (Genesis 41:16-38).

(3) **The Spirit helped the judges and rulers of God's people.** Divine guidance through the Spirit was given to: (1) Othniel (Judges 3:10); (2) Gideon (Judges 6:34-35); (3) Jepthah (Judges 11:29); Samson (Judges 13:25; 14:6; 15:14-15); and (5) David (II Samuel 23:2; I Samuel 16:13).

(4) **The Spirit also gave aid to certain individuals.** In Exodus 35:31, the Spirit gave aid to Bezalel in the work of the Tabernacle. The Spirit of God came mightily upon Saul (I Samuel 10:10, 11:6). Noah was a preacher of righteousness (I Peter 3:20-21; II Peter 2:5). A Prophet was a spokesman for God and, to be a spokesman for God, one had to be endowed by the Spirit. (Read I Peter 1:10-12.)

(5) To add further, we list the following passages to show how the Spirit of God helped the Prophets of God:

(a)   Moses as a leader and teacher (Numbers 11:24-30).
(b)   Balaam (Numbers 24:2-9).
(c)   David (Psalm 51:11; also, Acts 2:30 and I Samuel 16:13).
(d)   Isaiah (Isaiah 6:1).
(e)   Ezekiel (Ezekiel 11:5).
(f)   Micah (Micah 3:8).
(g)   Nehemiah (Nehemiah 9:30).

However, it would certainly be in order to notice that, even though the Spirit was with them to guide, assist, and aid, the Spirit could be taken from them. Such was the possibility in the life of:

(a)　　Samson (Judges 13:25, 16:20).
(b)　　Saul (I Samuel 10:10, 16:14).
(c)　　David (Psalm 51:11,13).

The Old Testament is a vital part of our study concerning the Spirit of God. We see the Spirit of God at work in creation along with the other members of the Godhead. And we have seen the Holy Spirit at work in the lives of individuals to reveal God's will or to guide, assist, aid, and strengthen them to do God's biddings. Our understanding of the Spirit becomes clearer with a knowledge of His activity in the Old Testament.

The Holy Spirit in the New Testament:

The New Testament presents a much fuller revelation regarding the Holy Spirit than the Old Testament. The Spirit's activities, His advent, work, relation to Christ and the church are all discussed in the New Testament. There are approximately 264 references to the Holy Spirit in the New Testament. Names by which the Spirit is called are:

1. The Spirit (Romans 8:13).
2. Spirit of God (Romans 8:14).
3. Spirit of Christ (Romans 8:9).
4. The Spirit himself (Romans 8:16).
5. Spirit of God's Son (Galatians 4:6).
6. Spirit of the Father (Matthew 10:20).
7. Spirit of Truth (John 14:15-17).
8. Holy Spirit (Acts 28:25).
9. Comforter (John 14:26).

Regarding the Spirit and His relation to the New Testament, we note:

"The dispensation of the Spirit is clearly seen in the New Testament, and for this reason the New Testament may well be called 'The book of the Holy Spirit.' The Old Testament writers were aware of the Spirit's action upon inanimate nature and they attributed any unusual manifestation of power of a human spirit to an intervention of the Spirit of God. The New Testament writers, however, make it evident that the Holy Spirit was not only the channel for abnormal manifestations of spiritual power, but in New Testament times and during the age of the church would remain with man as an abiding source of life and as the agent of righteousness."[3]

To further show the emphasis given to the Spirit in the New Testament, we mention that the Spirit is referred to 12 times in Matthew, 6 times in Mark, 18 times in Luke, 23 times in John, 57 times in Acts, and 132 times in the Epistles through Revelation. Boles points out, "of the twenty-seven books in the New Testament, twenty-four make reference to the Spirit." The only books that don't mention the Spirit are Philemon and II and III John.

Figures and Symbols of the Holy Spirit:

As the New Testament speaks of the Holy Spirit, it also employs figures and symbols to describe Him. The Spirit is described as a **dove** at the baptism of Jesus in the River Jordan (Matthew 3:16). In I John 2:20-21, the Holy Spirit is referred to as an **anointing oil.** Ephesians 1:13-14 refers to the Holy Spirit as a **seal** and an **earnest of our inheritance.** In John 4:11, He is referred to as **water** and, in John 7:37-39, the Spirit is called **living water.** Another symbol ascribed to the Spirit is used by Jesus in Acts 1:5 as **being baptized in the Holy Spirit.** And Paul speaks in I Corinthians 12 about the **gifts of the Spirit.**

The Holy Spirit in the Life of Christ:

The Holy Spirit played a very important and active part in the life of Christ. Actually, the work of the Spirit in Christ's life began prior to the birth of Jesus.

The time of the coming of Christ was clearly and frequently foretold; he was to come 'in the latter days,' or at the end of the Mosaic dispensation (Isaiah 2:2). Again, it was foretold that he would come during the existence of the second temple; that is, while the second temple was standing (Malachi 3:1). He was to be born in Bethlehem of Judea (Micah 5:2). He was to come through the tribe of Judea (Genesis 12:3; Hebrews 2:16, 7:14).

He was to be in the line of David (Isaiah 11:10). The Holy Spirit foretold all of these and many other things concerning the Christ.[6]

The Holy Spirit's Work in the Birth of Christ:

Matthew's account of what happened when Mary conceived Jesus is as follows:

"Now the birth of Jesus Christ was on this wise: When his mother Mary had been betrothed to Joseph, before they came together she was found with child of the Holy Spirit. And Joseph her husband, being a righteous man, and not willing to make her a public example, was minded to put her away privily. But when he thought on these things, behold, an angel of the Lord appeared unto him in a dream, saying, "Joseph, thou son of David, fear not to take unto thee Mary thy wife: for that which is conceived in her is of the Holy Spirit' (Matthew 1:18-20).

(1).The work of the Holy Spirit in the life of Christ. The Spirit was given to Christ and continued with Him throughout his ministry:

(a) The Spirit given to Jesus at His baptism (Matthew 3:16; Mark 1:10; Luke 3:22).
(b) The Spirit being with Him during His temptation (Matthew 4:1; Mark 1:12).
(c) Jesus returned to Galilee in the power of the Spirit (Luke 4:14).
(d) Jesus was full of the Holy Spirit (Luke 4:1).

(2). The Spirit was with Christ in His work.

(a).The Spirit was with Christ (Isaiah 42:1-4; Matthew 12:15-21).
(b).The Spirit aided Christ to cast out demons (Matthew 12:28).
(c).Christ preached by the Spirit (Luke 4:18-21).
(d).Christ rejoiced in the Spirit (Luke 10:21).

(e). Christ gave commands by the Holy Spirit (Acts 1:2).

(3). The Holy Spirit was with Christ in His death and **resurrection.** Jesus offered Himself as a sacrifice for the sins of the world. This was His purpose in coming to the earth (John 1:29; Mark 10:45; Matthew 26:28; I John 2:2; Revelation 1:5; Acts 20:28; et al.). His offering of Himself was done freely (John 10:17). But Jesus offered Himself through the eternal Spirit (Hebrews 9:14). The Spirit aided Christ in His death on the cross.

The Scriptures continue and testify that the Spirit not only helped Christ in His death but also in His resurrection from the dead. (Read Romans 1:4; I Peter 3:18.) And it was by the power from the Spirit that Peter proclaimed His ascension and coronation on the first Pentecost following the Resurrection (Acts 2:33-36).

To summarize, we see that the Holy Spirit was always with Christ. The Spirit was there at His (a) birth, (b) life, (c) death, and (d) resurrection. Surely, we must give praise to God for the work of the Spirit in the life of Christ.

The Holy Spirit in the Gospel of John:

In a study of the Holy Spirit in the New Testament, we must consider what is said about the Spirit in John's Gospel. Much teaching is given in the Gospel of John concerning the Holy Spirit:

(1) The Spirit is at Jesus' baptism (John 1:32-33).

(2) The Spirit is referred to in Jesus' conversation with Nicodemus (John 3:1-8).

(3) The Spirit is given to Christ without measure (John 3:34).

(4) The Spirit is promised to all Christians after Jesus' glorification (John 7:38-39).

(5) Power from the Spirit is granted to the Apostles to grant forgiveness (John 20:22-23).

This discussion, however, will be concerned with the private ministry of Jesus when He was alone with His disciples apart from the masses. The record is found in chapters 14-16. In this section of

Scripture, there are **five major sayings.** Within these five major sayings, at least seven thoughts emerge. Each of these is worthy of our consideration.

(1) The First Saying—John 14:16-17, "And I will pray the Father and he shall give you another Comforter, that he may be with you forever, even the Spirit of truth: whom the world cannot receive; for it beholdeth him not, neither knoweth him: ye know him: for he abideth with you, and shall be in you." In this saying comes three thoughts:

(a) **Another Comforter**—This is the same word used of Jesus in I John 2:1 and is translated **advocate.** The term refers to a person who is called to the side of another in order to help. In being another Comforter, the Holy Spirit will comfort, teach, guide, and testify. Thus, there are two helpers: Christ in heaven and the Spirit on earth.

(b) **The Spirit of Truth**—This is the Spirit **which is truth;** truth in His person. The Spirit teaches the truth as He gives the Word to the Apostles. The world follows Satan (falsehood), but the Christian follows Christ and His Spirit (truth).

(c) **The Indwelling Spirit**—Notice the language: (a) The Spirit was to be "with" them (John 14:16); and (b) The Spirit was to be "in" them (John 14:17).

(2) The Second Saying—John 14:25-26, "These things have I spoken unto you, while yet abiding with you. But the Comforter, even the Holy Spirit, whom the Father will send in my name, he shall teach you all things, and bring to your remembrance all that I said unto you."

(d) **A Teacher**—Jesus reveals another work of the Spirit when He states that the Spirit would teach them all things. The Spirit acted as a teacher to the Apostles as Jesus had also done while with them. A part of this teaching was to bring to their remembrance things He Himself had taught them. The immediate application is to the Apostles, and we receive the benefit of this blessing to the Apostles through a study of the Scriptures.

(3) The Third Saying—John 15:26-27, "But when the Comforter is come, whom I will send unto you from the Father, even the Spirit of truth which proceedeth from the Father, he shall bear witness of me: and ye also bear witness, because ye have been with me from the beginning." In the preceding verses, Jesus has spoken of the world hating both Him and His disciples. However, Jesus says the Comforter (Holy Spirit, John 14:16) will help them and bear witness of Him.

(e) **Witness**—This bearing witness is the fifth thought we gain from the passages under consideration. The word "witness" means to confirm or attest to the truthfulness of something.

As the disciples face tribulation and trials, the Spirit will bear witness to the truth concerning Jesus Christ.

(4) The Fourth Saying—John 16:7-11, "Nevertheless I tell you the truth: it is expedient for you that I go away; for if I go not away, the Comforter will not come unto you. And he, when he is come, will convict the world in respect of sin, and of righteousness, and of judgment: of sin, because they believe not on me; of righteousness, because I go to the Father, and ye behold me no more; of judgment because the prince of this world hath been judged." In this saying, Jesus says it is best for Him to go away so the Comforter will come. The work of the Comforter will be to convict the world in respect of sin, righteousness, and judgment to come. Conviction comes as a result of preaching. Conviction coincides with reprove, rebuke, convince, or expose. The Spirit, through preaching, did that on Pentecost as Peter preached. He convicted them of: (a) Sin—they had rejected Christ;

(b) Righteousness—Christ was a man approved of God; and

(c) Judgment—"Save yourselves from this crooked generation."

(5) The Fifth Saying—John 16:12-15, "I have yet many things to say

unto you, but ye cannot bear them now. Howbeit when he, the Spirit of truth, is come, he shall guide you into all the truth: for he shall not speak from himself; but what things soever he shall hear, these shall he speak: and he shall declare unto you the things that are to come. He shall glorify me: for he shall take of mine, and shall declare it unto you. All things whatsoever the Father hath are mine: therefore said I, that he taketh of mine, and shall declare it unto you." In this fifth saying, the seventh thought that we wish to study is found: "And he shall declare unto you things to come" (John 16:13). The thought injected here is found in the word "prophecy." Perhaps the better word would be "prediction" (to tell future events), because "prophecy" doesn't always demand a foretelling of future events.

To conclude the work of the Holy Spirit in John's Gospel, we summarize that in the five sayings, there are seven works of the Spirit mentioned:

(1) Comforter.
(2) Spirit speaks truth.
(3) Indwells.
(4) Teaches.
(5) Witness.
(6) Convicts.
(7) Prophesies or Predicts.

Conclusion:

We have seen an overview of the Holy Spirit in relation to both the Old and New Testaments. The Spirit of God plays an important part in the lives of God's people. Of special interest to us are the passages of scripture that refer to the Holy Spirit in the life of the person under the New Covenant—the Christian. A study of this will follow in the next chapter. This study is not exhaustive. There are perhaps many passages or incidents that others would have referred to if they were doing the writing. We do hope, however, that this "bird's-eye" view of the Holy Spirit in relation to the Testaments will increase our understanding and appreciation of this important member of the Godhead.

QUESTIONS FOR DISCUSSION

1. Discuss the work of the Holy Spirit in creation.
2. Discuss the distinction between God and the Spirit of God.
3. What work did the Spirit do in lives of the people during Old Testament times?
4. What names are given to the Holy Spirit in the Old Testament? New Testament?
5. Discuss the figures used in describing the Holy Spirit in the New Testament.
6. Was the Holy Spirit active in the Life of Christ? What did He do?
7. Is it true that the Holy Spirit left Jesus in Christ's death on the cross? Discuss.
8. Explain Hebrews 9:14.
9. List and discuss the seven works of the Holy Spirit in the five sayings found in the Gospel of John.
10. What part did the Holy Spirit play in the creation of man?
11. What was the Spirit's work in relationship to Divine Revelation (the Bible)? (Read and discuss II Peter 1:20-21.)

FOOTNOTES

[1]Garth W. Black, *The Holy Spirit* (Abilene, TX: Biblical Research Press, 1967), p. 11.

[2]Richard Rogers, "The Holy Spirit" (unpublished paper, 1968), p. 9.

[3]Black, p. 16.

[4]Black, p. 16.

[5]H. Leo Boles, *The Holy Spirit* (Nashville, TN: Gospel Advocate Co., 1942), p. 63.

[6]Ibid., p. 12

Chapter Thirteen
THE HOLY SPIRIT TODAY
Introduction

The promise of the Holy Spirit as prophesied by Joel, in Joel 2:28-32, has been fulfilled. Peter, by inspiration of the Spirit, stood on Pentecost and proclaimed, "this is that which was spoken by the prophet Joel" (cf. Acts 2:16ff). The Holy Spirit was now carrying out His mission to convict the world of sin and of righteousness and of judgment to come. Peter preached the word given him by the Holy Spirit. Three thousand were convicted of their sins and cried out, "men and brethren what shall we do?" The Holy Spirit gave the answer, "Repent and be baptized." We, too, can convict the world of sin when we preach the words of the Spirit recorded for us in the Word of God. This lesson will give a study of the subject of the Holy Spirit today.

The Gift of the Holy Spirit:

Much controversy is aroused by the phrase used by Peter the apostle on the day of Pentecost when he said in Acts chapter 2, verse 38, "repent and be baptized every one of you, in the name of Jesus Christ unto the remission of your sins; and ye shall receive the gift of the Holy Spirit." In this portion of our study, we want to consider what is meant by the phrase "the gift of the Holy Spirit."

Let's begin by looking at Peter's Words:

(1) **The commands Peter preached.** Peter commanded those who believe to do two things: first, he said they must "repent" and, second, he said they must "be baptized." This was not the first time these two subjects were mentioned. These commandments are found also in Luke 13:3,5, Luke 24:44-47, Mark 16:16, and Matthew 28:18-2.0.

(2) **Peter made two promises to those who are obedient: (a) the remission of sin, and (b) the gift of the Holy Spirit.** Peter's promise of the blessing of the remission of sins and the gift of the Holy Spirit

was for all, just as the commandment to repent and be baptized is for all. Peter continues, "for the promise is unto you [that is, the Jews assembled there] and to your children [that is, to their descendants] and to them that are afar off [that is, the promise to the Gentiles also, cf. Ephesians 2:11-13] and as many as the Lord our God shall call (Acts 2:39)." Now a man who accepts the call of the gospel (II Thessalonians 2:14) and is obedient to it, and repents of sins and is baptized into Christ, receives the forgiveness of sins and the gift of the Holy Spirit." William Banowsky observed,

There is no more thrilling message in all the Bible than these words of a **promise**. With this **promise,** the apostle Peter concluded his epoch-making address at Pentecost. And with this **promise,** the Christian religion ceased to be mere theory and became reality in the lives of several thousand who "gladly received the Word." [1]

This promise that Peter made of the gift of the Holy Spirit seems to cause considerable question from some people. When Peter spoke of the "gift of the Holy Spirit," was he referring to some special blessings that were to be received from the Holy Spirit? Or was he referring to the gift of the Spirit Himself?

We believe that the phrase "the gift of the Holy Spirit" refers to the Spirit Himself as a gift that is available to all men today who submit to the commandments that preceded the promise of this gift. Reasons for such a conviction are:

(1) **The Bible says the Spirit is a gift from God** (I Thessalonians 4:8; Romans 5:5; Acts 2:38; 5:32).

(2) **The Bible says the gift of the Spirit is God's certification that one is a Son.** "In whom ye also, having heard the word of the truth, the gospel of your salvation, whom, having also believed, ye were sealed with the Holy Spirit of promise" (Ephesians 1:13). The word **seal** is a very interesting word. Official papers or documents are stamped with a seal. This seal certifies that the document is authentic and genuine and respected as such by the

proper authorities. Seals have been used for some time. As a matter of fact, they were used in ancient times and were found in the form of cylinder-shaped or carved-on rings, and were used to make official impressions on clay tablets.

When we (1) heard the word of truth, the gospel, and (2) believed it, (3) repented of our sin, and (4) were baptized into Christ, God gave us the gift of the Holy Spirit that certifies that we are His property.

(3) **The Bible says that the gift of the Holy Spirit is an "earnest" of our inheritance (Ephesians 1:14). The word earnest is a word** which means "down payment." Earnest money is the money given in pledge of making the full purchase of a given possession at a later date. The Holy Spirit is given to the Christian and serves as God's pledge for the inheritance that God has promised.

(4) **The Bible says that without the Spirit, we are not Christ's.** "But if any man hath not the Spirit of Christ, he is none of His" (Romans 8:9).

From the preceding, it is seen that the possession of the Holy Spirit is necessary for the Christian. The following men commented about this phrase in this manner:

(1) **J. W. McGarvey**—"The second blessing promised on condition of repentance and baptism, is the 'gift of the Holy Spirit.' By this is not meant that miraculous gift which had been bestowed upon the Apostles; for we know from the subsequent history that this gift was not bestowed on all who repented and were baptized, but on only a few brethren of prominence in the several congregations. The expression means the Holy Spirit as a gift; and the reference is to that indwelling of the Holy Spirit by which we bring forth the fruits of the Holy Spirit, and without which we are not of Christ. Of this promise Peter speaks more fully in the next sentence of his sermon."

(2) **H. Leo Boles**—"It should be remembered that there is a clear

and definite distinction to be made between the Holy Spirit as a gift and the gifts of the Holy Spirit. The Holy Spirit, when received, may be spoken of as a gift. In fact, Peter so speaks of the Holy Spirit as a gift... The gift of the Holy Spirit as a phrase is found only twice in the New Testament (Acts 2:38 and 10:45). However, it seems to have a different connotation in each use of the phrase.

In Acts 2:38, the apostle seems to have in mind that gift that belongs to all Christians, while in Acts 10:46, he has reference to the baptism of the Holy Spirit." [3]

(3) **Garth W. Black**—"The true meaning of the 'gift of the Holy Spirit' can be seen from a study of the New Testament passages that teach the Holy Spirit has been given to the Christian and dwells within him. In Paul's letter to the church at Rome there are several passages which show that the Holy Spirit dwells in the Christian. 'The love of God hath been shed abroad in our hearts through the Holy Spirit which was given unto us' (Romans 5:5). Again, 'But if the Spirit of him that raised up Christ Jesus from the dead dwells in you, he who raised Christ Jesus from the dead shall give life also to your mortal bodies through His Spirit that dwelleth in you' (Romans 8:11). And then in Paul's first epistle to the Corinthians, 'Or know ye not that your body is a temple of the Holy Spirit which is in you, which ye have from God? and ye are not your own?' (I Corinthians 6:19)."

Therefore, we see that the Bible testifies to the **fact** that the Holy Spirit is a gift that is given to the Christian to dwell within him. This leads to our next portion of study.

The Indwelling of the Holy Spirit:

In Romans 8:9-11, Paul states that the Holy Spirit dwells in Christians. "But ye are not in the flesh, but in the Spirit, if so be that the Spirit of God dwelleth in you. Now if any man hath not the Spirit of Christ, he is none of His." The apostle John also states, "Hereby we know that He abideth in us, by the Spirit which he gave us" (I John 3:24). And again, "Hereby we know that we abide in Him, and He in us, because He hath given us of His Spirit" (I John 4:13). The language seems to be very clear. The Bible says that the Spirit dwells in the Christian.

Concerning the indwelling of the Holy Spirit, one writer outlines it this way:

(1) The promise of it—
(a) Ezekiel 36:27, 37:14, 39:29; Isaiah 44:3; Joel 2:28; Zechariah 12:10.
(b) Luke 11:13; John 7:38-39, 14:16-17,23.
(2) The place of it—
(a) "within you"—Ezekiel 36:27, 37:14; John 14:16—16:23.
(b) "In the body"—I Corinthians 6:19-20.
(c) "In the heart"—Galatians 4:6.
(d) "In the belly"—John 7:38-39.
(3) The provision of it—
(a) Received at baptism—Acts 2:38.
(b) Comes by hearing of faith—Galatians 3:2.
(c) Given to those who obey—Acts 5:32.
(d) Given because they are sons—Galatians 4:6; 3:26-27.
(e) He is God's gift—I Thessalonians 4:8 (cf. Acts 2:38, 5:32).'

These facts need to be kept before us as we consider the indwelling of the Holy Spirit of God:

(1) The Holy Spirit is a gift from God (Acts 2:38, 5:32; I Thessalonians 4:8; Romans 5:5).
(2) Our bodies are a temple of the Holy Spirit (I Corinthians 6:19-20).
(3) The Holy Spirit is proof of sonship (Romans 8:14-16; Galatians 4:6; Romans 8:9).

Various writers have commented on the subject of the indwelling Spirit. The following is presented for your consideration:

(1) **Moses E. Lard**—"But what kind of dwelling is the last? Let the language be understood. When it is said that the Holy Spirit dwells in Christians not actually and literally, but merely through the truth representatively, the implication clearly is, that the Spirit itself does not dwell in them at all. On the contrary, the truth only dwells in them, and this stands for or is in the place of the Spirit. This unquestionably is the meaning of the language.

That the Holy Spirit actually and literally dwells in Christians is undisputably affirmed in the word of God; and hence cannot be rejected..."

(2) **J. W. McGarvey** (commenting on Acts **2:38**)—"The expression means the Holy Spirit by which we bring forth the fruits of the Spirit, and without which we are not of Christ."

(3) **James D. Bales**—"We should accept the fact of the indwelling of the Spirit, but we should not try to explain it in such a way as to commit us to an unscriptural position. In fact, since God has not revealed an explanation, we cannot know that any human explanation is right. Faith not only accepts what God has revealed, but it is content to leave matters where the Bible leaves matters. Since, so far as the author knows, the Bible does not give us any details on how the Spirit dwells in us—though it gives us the conditions—we must accept the fact and be content to be left without an explanation of how it is done. Faith does not look to some inner voice for instruction. Instead it relies upon what the Spirit has spoken to us through the written Word (Comp. Revelation 2:1,7).

To refuse to listen to the Word, or to be indifferent to the Word, is to be indifferent to the Spirit, for the Word is the word of the Spirit.

If the Bible stated that the Holy Spirit dwells in us representatively in that His word dwells in us, we would accept this; but the Bible does not so state, so far as the author knows."

(4) **J. W. Roberts**—"In this first article we have affirmed our belief in

the real, personal indwelling of the Holy Spirit in the body of the Christian. We believe that the Biblical references to this fact must be taken literally and not as metaphors or metonymy. The indwelling of the Hol^ Spirit had nothing to do with miracle working or revelation."

There are basically **six major theories on how** the Holy Spirit dwells in the Christian. Essentially, they are as follows:

(1) That the Spirit dwells in us only in the attitudes of our mind (modernist attitude).
(2) **That the Spirit dwells in us, the church, corporate, and not individually.** (The Spirit does dwell in the church as a corporate body, but not alone in this manner.)
(3) **That the Spirit dwells in us only as we have the word of God in us—that He dwells through the word, and that alone.** (But if we say the Spirit dwells in us only through the word, we say that the Spirit does not dwell in us at all, only the word dwells in us.)
(4) That we can know the Spirit indwells in us by performing miraculous gifts, such as the modern faith healers. (This is false!)
(5) That the Spirit dwells in us personally, separate and apart from the Word, but only works through the Word. (This position rejects a direct operation.)
(6) That the Spirit dwells in us in some sense, but we do not know how. (We need passages for all we teach.)

A person who does not believe in the indwelling of the Spirit of God runs into problems that cause great difficulties. Some questions that need to be answered are:

(1) If we are not to take the passages about the indwelling to mean what they say, then how are we to take them?
(2) Why would one go to great lengths to explain away a clear Biblical statement?
(3) Does the Bible deny a personal indwelling of the Spirit?
(4) Is it possible for the Holy Spirit to dwell in us?

(5) **If** the Spirit and the word are the **same,** what passages teach it?
(6) If we believe the Spirit dwells in us, does this automatically mean we must feel it?
(7) Did the Spirit dwell in two persons at the same time in New Testament times?
(8) Which plain passage teaches that the Spirit dwells only through the word?
(9) Why ask "how" does the Spirit dwell?

Roy Lanier, Sr., presents the following in favor of the indwelling of the Holy Spirit:

The Holy Spirit dwells in us (Acts 2:38; Romans 8:9-11; I Corinthians 6:19; II Corinthians 1:22):
(1)   Personally.
(a) Apostles (John 14:17) "He abideth with you" in person of Son. "Shall be in you" in his own person.
(b) Corinthians (I Corinthians 6:19) "In you."
(2)   Not through the word.
(a) Received the word before baptism, Spirit after (Acts 2:41).
(b) Hear and believe before we receive the Spirit (Ephesians 1:13).
(c) Sons of God before receiving the Spirit (Galatians 4:6). [10]

Under the topic **"Does the Holy Spirit dwell in us?"** brother Gus Nichols quotes Acts 2:38, Acts 5:32, Romans 8:9-10, I Corinthians 3:16, I Corinthians 6:19, I Thessalonians 4:8, Jude 19, and Ephesians 1:13; then, he states,

These are a few of the scriptures which teach that we, as Christians, have the Holy Spirit dwelling in us. Upon this fact we should all be united, as we have been ever since 1 have been a member of the church. However, there are some who hold theories which logically would deny that the Holy Spirit now dwells in us at all, that is, in any real sense. [11] With this in mind, one question is asked: "How can I know that the Spirit of God dwells in me?" Regardless of what some people say, a person **cannot know** of the indwelling of the Spirit:

(1) By a strange feeling or something that the Spirit does to him;
(2) By hearing a still small voice;
(3) By a miraculous sign;
(4) Because some man tells him so; or
(5) By a direct operation.

But, a person **can know** that the Holy Spirit dwells in him:
(1) Because of plain Bible passages that teach it;
(2) Because he accepts it by faith (Galatians 3:14; Hebrews 11:1,6; Romans 10:17).
(3) And by seeing the fruit of the Spirit in his life and the life of other Christians (Galatians 5:22-24; Ephesians 5:8-10).

Results of the Indwelling Holy Spirit:

The result of the indwelling Spirit is of vital importance to our study. This is looking at the why of the Spirit's indwelling. Why does the Holy Spirit dwell within me? The following Biblical evidence is presented in answer to that question.

(1) **The Holy Spirit dwells in the Christian to represent the dwelling of Deity within** (I John 4:12-15; II Corinthians 6:16; Ephesians 3:17 and 2:22). Moses Lard wrote, "The Holy Spirit dwelt in the saints in Ephesus, and by it, as representing Him, God dwelt in them." [12]

(2) The Holy Spirit dwells in the Christian as a proof of his sonship **(Galatians 4:6; Romans 8:9).**

(3) The Holy Spirit dwells in the Christian to be a seal of salvation and an earnest of his inheritance (Ephesians 1:13-14; Romans 8:23; II Corinthians 1:22; Ephesians 4:30).

(4) **The Holy Spirit dwells in the Christian to serve as a motivation to Godly living** (I Corinthians 6:19). If the Spirit of God dwells within me, it should cause me to be extra careful to see to it that nothing defiles the temple in which the Spirit of God dwells. Our body, because of the presence of the Holy Spirit, has become a

"holy of holies," a dwelling place for God through His Spirit.6
(5) The Holy Spirit dwells in the Christian and makes intercession for him before the throne of God (Romans 8:26-27).

The Holy Spirit and Conversion:

Conversion, whenever it takes place, is begun, directed, and completed by the power of the Holy Spirit through the word. Paul mentions the "renewing of the Holy Spirit" (Titus 3:5-6) and of the "new birth" being "from above" (John 3:3-5). The question at hand for us is: "How does the Holy Spirit work in conversion today?"

Many people think the Holy Spirit converts by performing a "direct operation" on the heart of the alien sinner. Most who hold this persuasion believe that a man is totally depraved in heart and soul and must have an operation on his heart directly from God to turn him from sin. However, the Bible teaches that the Spirit operates on the heart of the alien sinner through the agency of the written word of God.

Man is saved by grace through faith (Ephesians 2:8-10). Faith comes from hearing the Word of God (Romans 10:17). Thus, as man hears the word of God, believes and obeys it, the Spirit convicts him of sin and converts him to God. A careful study of the book of Acts shows that the Spirit converts through the word as the word is preached. Notice:

ACTS
(1) The Three Thousand .... "when they **heard** this"—2:37-38.
(2) The Five Thousand "many **heard** the **word,** believed"—4:4.
(3) The Samaritans .... "they believed Philip **preaching**"—8:12.
(4) Simon .... **"believed** also"—8:13.
(5) The Treasurer ..... "Philip **preached** unto him Jesus"—8:35-38.

---

6 This does not warrant the conclusion, which some have made, that man should be worshipped since the Holy Spirit dwells in him. Peter rejected worship (Acts 10:25-27), and who would deny that the Spirit indwelt him?

(6) Saul of Tarsus .... "shall be **told** thee what to do"— 9:6.
(7) Cornelius................ **"Words** whereby thou shalt be saved"— 11:14.
(8) Lydia .... **"heard,**attended to things **spoken"**— 16:14.
(9) Jailor .... **"Spake** unto him the **Word"**— 16:32.
(10) The Corinthians..... **"hearing,** believed, were baptized"—18:8.
(11) The Bereans .... **"Received**the Word"— 17:12.
(12) The Twelve............ "When they **heard** this, were baptized"— 19:5.

God's Word is active and sharper than any two-edged sword (Hebrews 4:12). It is the sword of the Spirit (Ephesians 6:14). This sword wields a powerful influence on the hearts of men and thereby effects conversion in their lives.

A **direct operation** of the Holy Spirit in conversion contradicts plain Biblical teaching. Consider carefully the following questions:

(1) If the Holy Spirit operates in conversion in a direct way, apart from the written word of God, then why are there some lands where there are no Christians? Is the Spirit failing to do His work?

(2) If the Spirit operates directly in conversion, why are some converted and others not? Is God a respecter of persons, sending His Spirit only to a certain select few?

(3) Where does the Bible record the Spirit operating in conversion directly on the heart of the alien sinner?

(4) If men are converted without the scripture, how can we distinguish between the many different groups which all make the same claim and yet teach different doctrines?

(5) If the Spirit operates on man's heart, separate and apart from the written word of God, wouldn't this violate man's nature of

God allowing him to be a free moral agent and make a choice? The truth of the matter is—the Spirit of God works through the written word of God in converting men to Christ (Romans 1:16).

The Holy Spirit and the Word of God:

The relationship of the Holy Spirit to the Word of God is of importance in our study. The Spirit of God inspired the men who wrote the Bible (II Peter 1:20-21; 11 Timothy 3:16-17). The Word of God that was given through the Spirit is the instrument that the Spirit uses in conversion today. The Word of God is what governs the actions of Christians (1 Peter 4:11).

The Bible reveals that there are many cases in which the action of the Holy Spirit and the Word of God are the same.

(1) The Christian is born of the Holy Spirit (John 3:5-8) and the Word of God (I Peter 1:23).

(2) Man is saved by the Spirit (Titus 3:5) and by the Word of God (James 1:21).

(3) Man is sanctified by the Spirit (I Corinthians 6:11; 11 Thessalonians 2:13) and by the Word of God (John 17:17).

(4) The Spirit is Truth (I John 5:7) and the Word of God is Truth (John 17:17). However, this does not mean that the Word of God and the Holy Spirit are one and the same. The Word is the "sword of the Spirit" (Ephesians 6:17; cf. also Romans 8:26-27). The instrument through which the Spirit works is the truth of God: He works through **no other means** in the conversion of sinners and sanctification of saints.

Gifts from the Holy Spirit:

That the early church was endowed with special spiritual gifts cannot be open to discussion. Such passages as Romans 12:6-8, Acts 8:14-18, and I Corinthians, chapters 12 through 14, teach that such gifts were in existence in the infant days of the church. As we enter into this portion of our study, it must be emphasized that there is a definite distinction between the **gifts from the Holy Spirit** and the **gift of the Holy Spirit.** Christ is the giver of the Spirit, and the Spirit gives gifts to whomsoever He will (I Corinthians 12:11).

Gifts were given by the Spirit in the early church in two ways.

(1) **Directly**—This happened on two occasions in the New Testament:

   a. The Apostles on Pentecost (Acts 2:1-42); and (b) The house of Cornelius (Acts 10:44-46).

(2) **Indirectly**—Through the laying on of the Apostle's hands, miraculous gifts from the Spirit could be passed on to others. This happened with: (a) The Samaritans (Acts 8:4-19); (b) The Ephesians (Acts 18:24—29:7); and (c) Timothy (II Timothy 1:6).

As gifts were given, not all received the same gift (cf. I Corinthians 12:4-11,13). There were different gifts given to different people (I Corinthians 12:11).

One important area of study is to see the purpose for the existence of such gifts. The Bible gives three reasons for spiritual gifts being given during the infant days of the church:

(1) Spiritual gifts were granted to the Apostles to serve as credentials of their Apostleship (II Corinthians 12:12; Acts 2:43, 5:12);

(2) Spiritual gifts were a means of showing that the message spoken by someone was trustworthy and from God (I Corinthians 14:12-26, 31); and

(3) Spiritual gifts were used to confirm the Word spoken (Mark 16:16-20; Hebrews 2:3-4). (Spiritual gifts were never used for personal gain or power.)

Regarding the use of spiritual gifts, it must also be observed that the Bible says that they were to cease. In 1 Corinthians 13:8, Paul states, "Love never faileth: but whether there be prophecies, they shall be done away; whether there be tongues, they shall cease; whether there be knowledge, it shall be done away." Notice the phrases "done away" and "cease."

Question: When were these gifts spoken of here to be done away or to cease? **Answer:** When they had accomplished that for which they were intended. Spiritual gifts were used to confirm the Word (Mark 16:20). A confirmation is a final act. Once something is confirmed, it need never be confirmed again. No one adds to or takes away from something that has been confirmed (cf. Galatians 3:15; Hebrews 6:16). To argue for the use of spiritual gifts today is to argue that we do not have the confirmed Word of

God. Yet, the Bible claims to be the confirmed Word of God (cf. Hebrews 2:2-4); we have all things pertaining to life and godliness (II Peter 1:3; Jude 3).

Tongue Speaking—Is it for Today?

Tongue speaking, commonly referred to as **glossolalia,** is one of the fastest growing trends in the religious world today. Its impact has been so great that it has even made its mark among members of the body of Christ.

In the New Testament, there are only 5 references made to "tongue speaking":

(1) Mark 16:17
(2) Acts 2
(3) Acts 10
(4) Acts 19
(5) I Corinthians 12-14.

"Acts records the history of the phenomena without regard to the assemblies of Christians, while Corinthians treats the phenomena relative to the assembly."

An examination of two of these passages of scripture is in order. The two we shall examine are Acts 2 and I Corinthians 14.

(1) Acts 2:1-11. (Read these verses!) This is the first record of "speaking in tongues" recorded as historically happening in the New Testament. From this section of scripture, Jimmy Jividen makes the following conclusions to show that the tongues spoken of were not "ecstatic languages" but were "spoken languages of

men." His conclusions are summarized as:

(a) The Apostles were speaking in tongues **(glossa)**, but they were speaking languages **(dialektos)**. The languages they spoke were not some heavenly unknown languages but were languages known by men. Verse 8 states, "And how hear we, every man in our own language wherein we were born?"

(b) The crowd that was gathered was amazed that these Galileans were speaking in languages that were not their own. "The marvel of it all was that men who were known to be of one dialect could fluently speak another language."

(c) There are some fifteen nationalities listed by Luke in connection with the "tongue speaking" in Acts 2. "These nationalities probably refer to Jews of the dispersion who no longer knew Aramaic. If languages of these nationalities were not meant, why would these different nationalities be mentioned? The different nationalities were saying, 'we hear them speaking in our tongues.' " [15]

(2) **I Corinthians 14.** (Read this chapter carefully!) In this chapter from Paul's epistle to the church at Corinth, we find speaking in tongues. This chapter says:

(a) Tongue speaking is addressed not to man but to God, verses 2 and 28.

(b) The person who speaks in a tongue speaks mysteries, verse 2.

(c) The tongue speaker edifies only himself and not those who hear him speaking in the tongue, verse 4.

(d) The tongue speakers understanding when praying in the Spirit is unfruitful, verse 14.

(e) The tongue speaking was not understood by the hearers, verse 19. Outsiders hearing everyone in the church speaking in tongues will think it is madness, verse 23.

In I Corinthians 14:21, Paul uses a quotation from Isaiah 28, in reference to tongue speaking. However, Isaiah was not speaking of ecstatic utterances, but of a foreign language. The apostle uses the context of the Isaiah passage to teach a lesson to the Corinthians. Just as the priests and prophets of Isaiah's day refused to hear the prophecy of Isaiah, the Corinthians did not care for the gift of prophecy. Just as those who rejected prophecy in Isaiah's day had to hear another language, the same was true of members of the church at Corinth.[16] (Remember, also, the word "unknown" is not in the original text.)

A Contrast Between New Testament and Modern Day Tongue Speaking:

Speaking in tongues in the New Testament and the modern day tongue speaking are quite different from one another. The contrast is really vast and unique. The following presents the contrast between the two:

(1) The New Testament gift of speaking in tongues was the gift of speaking a foreign language. The present day so-called tongue speaking occurrences are similar to those found in world religions and sometimes found outside religion altogether.

(2) The New Testament gift of speaking in tongues was used in the assembly and through the interpretation edified the church, but present day use of tongue speaking is used almost entirely for personal benefit and private devotion (1 Corinthians 14:23,5).

(3) The New Testament gift of speaking in tongues was received either directly from the Holy Spirit for a specific purpose or by the imposition of laying on of Apostles' hands. Present-day tongue speaking is "sought after" by various people who have an intense desire for the gift.

(4) The New Testament gift of speaking in tongues could be understood by men who spoke the language that the tongue speaker was speaking. Present day tongue speaking is "gibberish" and not understood by linguists.

(5) The New Testament gift of speaking in tongues (along with other

gifts) was used to confirm revelation from God. Present day tongue speaking has no new revelation to confirm.

(6) **The New Testament gift of speaking in tongues was temporary, and the gift was to cease.** Those today who claim to have the gift of speaking in tongues claim the gift is available for Christians of all ages. This is false!

Conclusion:

Our study has concerned itself with the work of the Holy Spirit today. We have affirmed that the Bible teaches that the Christian receives the gift of the Holy Spirit as a promise from God. This gift serves as a proof of one's sonship, a seal and an earnest of inheritance of eternal salvation. The Holy Spirit works in conversion through the written Word of God, but in no way endows men today with spiritual gifts as He did in the first century. Our final area of study dealt with tongue speaking, and we concluded that tongue speaking as it was known in the first century is entirely different from present day manifestations or claims to tongue speaking. We do not believe the Spirit endows men today with the gift of speaking in tongues (or any other miraculous gift), for that gift was to cease and there is no need for its existence today!

QUESTIONS FOR DISCUSSION

1. Discuss what is meant by the phrase "gift of the Holy Spirit."
2. Do you agree with the observation by William Banowsky concerning the **promise?** Why or why not?
3. Discuss the indwelling of the Holy Spirit in light of the biblical passages presented on the subject.
4. What are the six basic theories concerning the indwelling of the Holy Spirit?
5. List and discuss the results of the indwelling of the Holy Spirit.
6. How does the Holy Spirit work in converting men to Christ?
7. List the New Testament examples of how the Holy Spirit converted men.

8. What is the relationship that is sustained between the Holy Spirit and the Word of God?
9. Discuss the results of the position of a direct operation of the Holy Spirit in conversion.
10. Was the early church granted spiritual gifts from the Holy Spirit?
11. What were some of these gifts? List them.
12. How were spiritual gifts from the Spirit conferred upon men in the first Century? In what two ways? Give examples.
13. Present logical reasoning for believing that spiritual gifts have ceased.
14. Discuss the subject of tongue speaking. What observations from Acts 2 and I Corinthians 14 helped in your study of tongue speaking?
15. Contrast New Testament tongue speaking with the modern day claim to speaking in tongues.

FOOTNOTES

[1] William S. Banowsky, *The Gift of the Holy Spirit* (Fort Worth, TX: Fort Worth Christian College Lectures, 1964), p. 96.

[2] J. W. McGarvey, *A New Commentary On Acts Of Apostles* (Cincinnati, OH: Standard Pub. Co., no date), p. 39.

[3] H. Leo Boles, *The Holy Spirit* (Nashville, TN: Gospel Advocate Pub. Co., 1942), p. 171.

[4] Garth W. Black, *The Holy Spirit* (Abilene, TX: Biblical Research Press, 1967), pp. 33-34.

[5] Richard Rogers, "The Indwelling of the Holy Spirit" (unpublished paper from Lubbock, TX), p. 1.

[6] Moses E. Lard, *Lard's Quarterly* (March, 1964), Vol. 1, pp. 236-237.

[7] McGarvey, p. 39.

[8] James D. Bales, *The Holy Spirit* (Shreveport, LA: Gussie Lambert Publication, no date), p. 41.

[9] J. W. Roberts, *The Firm Foundation* (article dated January 25,

1967), p. 53.

[10]Roy Lanier, Sr., *The Holy Spirit* (Denver, CO: Bear Valley School of Preaching, no date), p. 7.

[11]"Gus Nichols, *Lectures on the Holy Spirit* (Plainview, TX: Nichols Brothers Publishers, 1967), pp. 157-158.

[12]Moses E. Lard, as quoted by Richard Rogers, "Outline on the Indwelling Spirit" (unpublished paper), p. 1.

[13]Jim McGuiggan, *Book of First Corinthians* (West Monroe, LA: Let the Bible Speak Publishers, 1973).

[14]Jimmy Jividen, *Glossolalia* (Fort Worth, TX: Star Bible Publications, 1971).

[15]Ibid., p. 37.

[16]Ibid., p. 40.

[17]Ibid., pp. 57-58.

CPSIA information can be obtained
at www.ICGtesting.com
Printed in the USA
LVHW041706210120
644288LV00016B/1756